Praise for *The CV Book*

'The essential toolkit for a winning CV!'
Lee Biggins, Founder and Managing Director of CV-Library

'A perfect and effective guide to getting your CV right, this book contains everything you will ever need to know about writing your CV.'
Steve Slocombe, Co-owner, GRS Recruitment

'James Innes' highly anticipated CV Book is an essential guide to building the right CV format in today's competitive and globalised marketplace. Innes packs his book with fascinating case studies, relevant questions and anecdotes, mistakes to avoid and most importantly, it provides an effective blueprint for creating an outstanding CV.'
Jorge Marcano, Strategic Communication Expert & Inter-Cultural Specialist, Multilingual HR Advisor at Barclays Lithuania

D0949102

The CV Book

The CV Book

How to avoid the most common mistakes and write a winning CV

Third edition

James Innes

Harlow, England • London • New York • Boston • San Francisco • Toronto • Sydney • Auckland • Singapore • Hong Kong
Tokyo • Seoul • Taipei • New Delhi • Cape Town • São Paulo • Mexico City • Madrid • Amsterdam • Munich • Paris • Milan

PEARSON EDUCATION LIMITED

Edinburgh Gate
Harlow CM20 2JE
United Kingdom
Tel: +44 (0)1279 623623
Web: www.pearson.com/uk

First published in Great Britain in 2009 (print)
Second edition published 2012 (print and electronic)
Third edition 2016 (print and electronic)

© James Innes 2009 (print)
© James Innes 2012, 2016 (print and electronic)

ISBN: 978-1-292-08647-7 (print)
       978-1-292-08649-1 (PDF)
       978-1-292-08648-4 (eText)
       978-1-292-08650-7 (ePub)

British Library Cataloguing-in-Publication Data
A catalogue record for the print edition is available from the British Library

Library of Congress Cataloging-in-Publication Data
A catalog record for the print edition is available from the Library of Congress

10 9 8 7 6 5 4 3 2 1
19 18 17 16

Cover design by redeyoffdesign.com
Cover image © Rodin Anton

Print edition typeset in 10pt/13pt Mundo Sans Pro by Lumina Datamatics
Printed in Malaysia (CTP-PJB)

NOTE THAT ANY PAGE CROSS REFERENCES REFER TO THE PRINT EDITION

Dedication

This book is dedicated to my parents. To my mother, Elisabeth, for teaching me everything that was ever of any real importance. To my father, Don, for guiding me and protecting me whilst always giving me the freedom to go my own way and find my own path in life.

Half of the author's royalties for this book will go to Durrell Wildlife Conservation Trust UK (registered charity number 1121989), a charity which supports conservation projects worldwide, continuing the work of the late, great Gerald Durrell, helping to save endangered species from extinction. **Up to 50 per cent of presently existing species face the possibility of becoming extinct by the end of this century.** I encourage my readers to join me in supporting this important cause. Donations can be made online at **www.justgiving.com/dwct**

Contents

About the author

James Innes is the founder and chairman of The CV Centre® – the UK's leading CV consultancy (**www.CVCentre.co.uk**) and part of the James Innes Group.

Following nearly two decades of experience heading up The CV Centre®, James is widely considered to be one of the UK's leading careers experts.

James regularly participates at recruitment fairs and conferences as a sought-after guest speaker, as well as being interviewed on TV and radio.

He is the author of a number of best-selling careers books. His current works are: *The CV Book, The Cover Letter Book, The Interview Book, The Interview Question & Answer Book* and *Ultimate New Job*.

Acknowledgements

I would like to thank all of my colleagues and clients at The CV Centre®, both present and past. Without them it would not have been possible for me to write *The CV Book*. In particular, I would like to thank our Chief Executive Officer, Andy Dalziel, and Managing Editor, Katy Wilson, especially for her assistance with the chapter on LinkedIn, as well as Jennifer David, Margaret Hall, Amanda Jones, Sean McAlister, Julie Sanders, Sharon Williamson and The CV Centre®'s former Director of UK Operations, Susan Staley.

I would additionally like to thank Richard Day, our former Director of Technology, and Peter Anders Hvass, our Chief Technology Officer, for their significant contributions to the online elements of this book. Also Kirk Hullis, our Chief Marketing Officer, for his work on the promotion of the book.

Special thanks also go to the team at Pearson, in particular Eloise Cook, Paul East, Katherine Habershon, Dhanya Ramesh and the editorial services team at Lumina Datamatics, Emma Steel and Natasha Whelan. I couldn't have had better publishers behind me.

Assistance in checking and correcting the text was also provided by Don Elkins, Elisabeth Elkins and Malcolm Innes.

Finally, I would like to thank my wife, Delphine Innes, and my daughter, Aleyna Innes, for their love and support and their toleration of my frequently working very excessively long hours! Je vous aime...

An apology in advance ...

It is impossible to write a book of this nature in such a way that all of the content will be perfectly suited to everyone. My readers range from manual workers to senior executives, to office workers and those who work in manufacturing and retail. There are those who work in a team, and those who don't. Some will have a boss; some will be the boss.

I've done my best to deliver a book which covers, as much as possible, all the different circumstances my readers might be in and all the different issues they might have to face. But there will inevitably be sections which don't apply to your own circumstances or where the focus is either above or below your level in the hierarchy. I can only apologise for this and hope you'll be kind enough to forgive me. My advice is to take what you need and to leave the rest.

How to use this book

There's no doubt about it; this book covers a lot of ground.

However, I appreciate that you may need to send your CV off later today and don't have the time to read everything. I have, therefore, provided a 'fast track' listing the top 15 questions that people ask me when writing a CV. This should help you to quickly and easily answer the vast majority of the points that may be troubling you.

Once you've found the answers to your questions and before finishing off your CV, make sure you spare five minutes to read Part 9: My five top tips to make your CV stand out. If you had time to read only two pages of *The CV Book*, these are the pages I would most like you to have taken the time to read. They encapsulate the most important principles that I cover in the book. Make an effort to accommodate all these when writing your CV and you'll immediately be well above average.

Writing a CV can be a lonely task. But you're not alone. There's someone I'd like to introduce you to.

Case study *Meet Jane Bloggs*

Throughout this book, I will be using a case study to better illustrate the ideas and principles and help bring them to life. This will also help you to better understand the issues raised and make it easier for you to apply the concepts to your own CV.

➤ Everyone is different and there is no one individual to whom all ideas will apply, but I have settled on an example which the majority of readers will be able to readily identify with. Meet Jane Bloggs!

➤ I won't tell you too much about her because we'll get to know her a lot better in the chapters to come. But, for now, I can tell you that Jane is 30 years old and works as a sales manager for a large stationery retailer, following previous experience in the food and drink sector. Having completed her BA (Hons) in Marketing and Advertising, she's keen to return to the food and drink sector and branch out into a combined sales and marketing role. She's also hoping that her next move will increase her level of responsibility and autonomy, and perhaps increase her pay packet!

The top 15 questions that people ask when writing a CV

If you're short on time and need answers fast then this section is for you.

Chances are you've got one or more of the following questions on your mind.

I have compiled this list based on the top 15 questions we most frequently get asked at The CV Centre® about CV writing. If you're reading this book, then it's more than likely that you will be asking yourself many of the same questions.

Each question is listed alongside details as to where in this book you can find the answers you are looking for.

All the answers to these questions and many more can be found within *The CV Book*. And if you have a question to which you can't find the answer, then why not visit our website: **www.jamesinn.es**

The top 15 questions

1 Which font do you recommend?
   Chapter 2 Aesthetics and presentation: looking good on paper
2 Should I use bullet points or full paragraphs?
   Chapter 3 Content and style: what to say and how to say it
3 Which type of CV should I use?
   Chapter 4 Structure: which type of CV is right for you?
4 How long should my CV be?
   Chapter 4 Structure: which type of CV is right for you?
5 What contact details should I put on my CV and where?
   Chapter 5 Personal details
6 Should I put my date of birth on my CV?
   Chapter 5 Personal details

PART 1

LAYING THE FOUNDATIONS: GETTING THE BASICS RIGHT

Chapter **1**

Why are CVs so important?

Dear Reader,

Why do some people almost always get the job they want?

Because *their* CV wins them an interview and 99 per cent *don't!*

As a professional CV writer, I see which CVs achieve results. This puts me in a unique position, enabling me to bring you the very best of what I have learned, helping you to create a truly exceptional CV.

What exactly is a 'curriculum vitae'?

'Curriculum vitae' is a Latin term and translates as 'the course of one's life'. The simplest definition is 'a summary of your academic and work history'. Well, that's basically true, but I see a curriculum vitae (CV) as more of a personal sales brochure, one which should be very carefully written and presented to ensure that you have the best possible chance of getting the job you want, to really showcase your talent.

It is not an autobiography. Simply writing down a list of everything you have done and everything you know will not guarantee you an interview; in fact, it will just bore the socks off the recruiter and undoubtedly count against you.

The primary aim of your CV is purely and simply to win you an interview.

What are the advantages of a properly presented and well-written CV?

It is vitally important to see matters from the recruiter's or prospective employer's perspective.

They're often faced with many hundreds of CVs to review for just one vacancy. Almost a third of recruiters admit to only reading a CV for a minute before deciding whether to interview the candidate. In fact, many admit to spending even less time! Twenty to 30 seconds is quite common.

They simply do not have the time to read them all in any depth. They're much more interested in getting out of the office and getting to the pub! In their initial sift they will be looking for reasons to discard your application, not for reasons to retain it. So how do you make your CV stand out? How do you maximise your chances of being among the ten or so candidates they decide to invite for interview?

My expertise in creating a truly professional CV is based on careful research into what recruiters really want from job applicants. This enables me to determine exactly what to put in and what to leave out, and what kind of a 'spin' to put on a CV to ensure that it will stand right out from the competition. Getting it right is the difference between getting your foot in the door for an interview, or ending up in the 'no thank you' pile – also known as the bin!

You need to help the recruiters as much as possible; they see sifting through CVs as a chore and want it to be over as quickly as possible (remember, there's that pint waiting for them down the road!). They do not know you and they don't know what you're capable of. This is where you have to sell yourself.

What can this book do to help you?

You're reading this book for one reason, to find out what makes an exceptional CV. You already realise just how important a document your CV is; it is probably the most important tool you will use during your job hunt, so getting it right is absolutely essential. It is also one of the few aspects of your job hunt that you are in full control of.

CV writing can be a tricky; it is part art, part science, and there is no one specific way that will suit everybody and every circumstance. However, in The CV Book I aim to demonstrate what you should and shouldn't do when writing your CV. No matter what your age, background, job or level of experience, I will help you to create a CV that really works for you.

This book condenses the same proven methodology I use every day with my clients and contains all the tips and – dare I say it – tricks that you need. I will cut through all the debate and opinion about CVs and show you what really works from the recruiter's point of view; what I have proved to work.

Thank you for choosing The CV Book. I have set out to write the most complete and up-to-date guide to CV writing on the market today; a definitive guide to CV writing. I trust that you will both enjoy it and find it useful. And I look forward to meeting you in cyberspace should you have any further questions.

I really want to help you get the job and the future that you want.

Kind regards,

James Innes

James Innes
Twitter: @jamesinnes
Chairman, The CV Centre®
Author:
The CV Book
The Cover Letter Book
The Interview Book
The Interview Question & Answer Book
Ultimate New Job

Chapter **2**

Aesthetics and presentation: looking good on paper

Presentation, presentation, presentation

The very first step you should take in creating your CV is to think about how you are going to present it. Most jobseekers don't realise that the way their CV is presented can often be of more value in getting to the next stage of the application process than the information in it. Presentation can make the difference between success and failure as it will make an impression on the reader even before they read a single word.

If the presentation of the CV is professional then the applicant gives the impression of being professional. But the opposite also applies: a poorly presented CV will give a poor impression of the applicant. You are marketing yourself, so the way you present your CV will have an impact on the reader that is almost as powerful as the content.

It is rare for me to come across a CV which couldn't benefit from some improvement to its presentation and layout. There's always at least one area that can be 'tweaked' to improve the visual impact of the CV – and often half a dozen!

Why is presentation so important?

Surveys show that badly presented and poorly written CVs are much more of a turn-off to recruiters than more obvious gaffs such as showing up late for interview or even swearing in an interview.

When faced with hundreds of CVs it's all too easy to just chuck a poor CV straight in the bin and that's the end of the story. However, when someone turns up for an interview, even if they don't make a great first impression, at least they've got their foot in the door. That's a significant advantage and yet another reason why getting your CV right is so important.

Good presentation can motivate the recruiter to read through your CV instead of someone else's and will instantly give them a positive feeling about you, whereas poor presentation may hide pertinent information you want the recruiter to see and could potentially ruin your chances of progressing to the interview stage. Your CV will more than likely end up in the bin (or possibly used as a paper dart!).

You may have spent many years obtaining skills and qualifications but if they are not presented effectively you won't achieve your career potential. This would be a terrible and unnecessary waste. But it's all too common.

Enhancing the presentation of a CV is very much the cosmetic surgery of the CV writing world. Content is clearly more important, and we'll go into this in more detail in the next chapter, but aesthetics are also critical in making the right impact on the reader. First impressions are absolutely vital as up to a quarter of CVs are immediately binned by recruiters because of poor presentation.

Typeface and font

Let's start with a couple of quick definitions for you.

The terms 'typeface' and 'font' are frequently conflated.

Typeface: a style of printed script, e.g. Times New Roman, Garamond, Arial or Helvetica.

Font: a subdivision of a typeface, e.g. bold or italic, including a denotation of size, traditionally measured in 'points'.

NB: these definitions are somewhat simplified but are more than sufficient for our purposes.

Typeface

I would recommend that you remain conservative with your choice of typeface.

Presentation is a personal issue and some people will prefer certain typefaces to others; for example, teachers often use Comic Sans. However, it is important to realise that the easiest-to-read typefaces will get you the positive presentation points! The CV Centre® generally uses mainstream typefaces such as Times New Roman, Garamond, Arial and Helvetica, as they are professional, easy to read and get results.

Avoid unusual typefaces, since they are generally harder to read, not only for humans but for automated scanning software. It is critical not to go over the top with fancy layouts or typefaces etc. They can detract and confuse. A clear, conservative impression is always preferable, except in specific cases such as architecture, graphic design etc., where you are entitled to demonstrate a little more creative licence.

I also need to define the difference between 'serif' and 'sans serif' typefaces.

A serif font has little flourishes or feet at the ends of some of the strokes that make up the letters and symbols within the typeface. And a sans serif font doesn't.

This is particularly noticeable on letters such as the capital W. But really the easiest way to describe this is to show you:

This is a serif typeface. And this is a capital W. (Times New Roman)

This is a sans serif typeface. And this is a capital W. (Arial)

Can you see the difference?

Serif fonts are generally recommended for text which is physically printed and read on paper as they are considered to increase readability.

Sans serif fonts, on the other hand, are usually recommended for electronic use.

It can be a good idea to prepare two different versions of your CV, one using a serif font (e.g. Times New Roman or Garamond) and one using a sans serif font (e.g. Arial or Helvetica). You can then use one for applications you make by post (if any!) and the other for applications you make online or via email.

Font

Bold: it's certainly a good idea to make use of bold type but it should be used sparingly to highlight headings and separate sections. It can also be used to draw the reader's eye towards key information; for example, degree titles. But avoid using it to highlight less important information, such as employers' names.

Italic: if you want to highlight particular sections of text then you should use bold, not italic. Italic should be used if you need to quote the names of publications, i.e. books, newspapers, magazines, journals etc. I also favour using it for your *Professional profile* and *Objective* (more about those later ...).

Size: try to keep to 11 or 12 point. You can make very limited use of 10 point and you can use 13 point or larger for main headings, including your name at the top of the CV. But the majority of the text should be either 11 or 12 point. And you should keep your headings consistent in size and the body copy consistent as well.

Break these rules at your peril. I have seen plenty of CVs where the writers have been so keen to cram everything in that they have resorted to 9 or 10 point throughout and the result is very tiring to read.

BLOOPER!

••

Some candidates are so desperate to fill up empty space that they use 14 point throughout. The resulting CV ends up looking like a book for toddlers!

Colour

You should only use black. In certain cases it can be acceptable to make limited use of colour, but the general rule is to stick to black. I once saw a CV that used four different colours, which is excessive. Your reader is expecting a black and white document, and whilst it can sometimes be good to stand out from the crowd, using colour to do so is not a technique I would recommend.

What is white space?

You need to carefully control your use of white space, presenting the information clearly and comprehensively and with style, within the limitations of the total space available.

'But what is white space?' I hear you ask.

'White space' is a term often used by designers to designate those parts of a page which are left blank (left white, i.e. not printed upon). Another commonly used and perhaps more meaningful term is 'empty space'. But I'm personally quite fond of the term 'breathing space' because that describes what white space is intended for, to give the reader some breathing space. It's not simply blank space; it's at least half of the document you are designing and getting the right balance between white space and non-white (or 'positive') space is vital if you are to maximise readability.

The key to using white space effectively is to realise that its purpose is:

➤ To provide 'breathing space' for the readers, so they are not overwhelmed with a solid block of hard-to-read text, and

➤ To group together related content and separate disparate content.

Space is at a premium when you are creating a CV. There's so much you have say, yet so little space to say it all in. But the key isn't to strip out the white space; instead, be highly selective and concise in terms of the content you include, and we'll discuss that in greater detail in later chapters. A page with minimal white space comes across as cluttered and difficult to read, which will definitely not help you get that job.

How to handle white space

White space includes your margins (top, bottom, left and right), line spacing, gaps between sections and tab spacing.

Like all design issues, spacing is subjective, and a CV that might appear cramped to one person may appear too widely spaced to another. You should endeavour to strike a balance.

Margins: keep them wide. The top margin shouldn't drop below 1.5 cm, nor should it exceed 3 cm; 2 cm–2.5 cm is perfect. The bottom margin should fall between 1 cm and 2 cm, although it is related to the top margin and should generally be 0.5 cm–1 cm smaller than the top margin. This is visually important. Left and right margins should remain within the range of 1.5 cm to 2.5 cm.

Header: the header should always start at least 1.25 cm from the edge because not all printers can print closer than 1.25 cm to the edge of a page.

Footer: the footer should also never start less than 1.25 cm from the edge. As for what to place in it, the footer simply needs to say 'Page 1 of x' even if the CV is only one page long. However, if you need to conjure up a little extra bit of room on a one-page CV, then it is also perfectly acceptable to replace the 'Page 1 of 1' with 'References are available on request'. This is a useful trick to get that little extra bit of space where needed.

In-text line spacing: you should always stick to standard single line spacing, rather than, for example, double line spacing.

Line spacing between sections: the ideal for this is 16 point. It is fine to use 14 point if space is short, but any less than this is to be avoided; it is far better to reduce the page margins or text size instead. A little more than 16 point is acceptable if required.

Justification: I recommend that the main text of your CV be fully justified. This means that it is aligned to both the left and right margins with extra space automatically added between words as necessary (like this book). It creates a nice clean look along both the left and right sides of the page. This is easy to achieve with word-processing software.

Beyond the first page: if your CV runs to more than one page then it's a good idea for the text on the second page (and subsequent pages if applicable) to start lower than that on the first. Given that you will be stapling the pages together, if the text on the second page starts too high up it'll be difficult to read because the staple will get in the way.

Readability

Readability is defined as the ease with which a reader can absorb the meaning of your words. The more readable your writing is, the more effectively it will communicate to your reader. Research shows that working to ensure readability can have a positive impact on comprehension, retention and reading speed, which in turn increases the chance that the reader will bother continuing to the end of the document.

We have already talked about the importance of selecting appropriate typefaces and controlling your use of white space, all of which contributes to a highly readable document.

But there's more to it than that.

You have another weapon up your sleeve....

Bullet points

In case you're not sure what bullet points (also known as simply 'bullets') are, they're the small dots, squares, dashes or arrows that can be used to introduce items in a list. For example:

- this is a bullet point
- and so is this.

In today's fast-paced world, recruiters no longer have the time to read large solid blocks of prose. They need to extract the information they need quickly. Long paragraphs are tiresome for a recruiter to read through, and many won't bother.

This is where bullet pointing comes in (although, unfortunately, many people fail to use it to their advantage within their CV). I wouldn't recommend you use bullet pointing everywhere; for instance, I wouldn't recommend using it for your *Professional* profile (see Chapter 6: Professional profile), but I would very strongly recommend its use in your *Career history*.

Some people worry that using bullet points will take up more room on their CV than writing in solid prose. Bullet points can potentially take up more room; however, if you word your CV carefully and concisely they shouldn't do so, and the positive impact on readability cannot be overstated.

How long should each bullet point be? Well, you should try to avoid bullet points that are only five or six words long. It's much better, visually, to aim for bullet points that at least fill the width of the page or even spill over onto a second line.

If you're faced with a stack of short bullet points then you should either rephrase them to increase the word count or amalgamate them with other bullet points so you end up with fewer longer bullet points.

TOP TIP

You should try to keep the length of your bullet-pointed lines more or less consistent. If they're all different lengths then it can look rather tatty.

Consistency of layout

A disorganised layout makes it hard for recruiters to extract the information they need.

Remember that most recruiters will be working under significant time pressure and so won't waste their time trying to pick out the information they need from a poorly organised layout. You'll end up in the bin.

The formatting you use for your CV should be consistent from beginning to end. Any inconsistencies should be carefully eliminated.

Many CVs have errors in formatting, which means that some lines are indented more than others and some sections have more space between them than others etc.

This just looks shoddy and communicates a pretty poor impression to the reader. If you can't be bothered to take the time to perfect your CV, then why should they be wasting their time reading it?

As well as consistency within the CV itself, if you are enclosing a cover letter with your CV (which you normally will be), both documents should match in style, ensuring a fully coordinated image. As the saying goes, image is everything.

Graphics

Computer software and the Internet make it very easy to quickly generate graphics, which you can then use in word-processed documents.

But just because it's easy to do doesn't necessarily mean that you should do it.

Should you, for example, include the logos of the organisations you have worked for?

Personally, I would advise against it as they can easily distract attention from the all-important content.

Good presentation is intended to make a document's content easier to read, not to usurp it.

You can use appropriate graphical devices such as plain horizontal lines to help separate different sections of your CV, but don't overdo it. The correct use of graphics is to help structure your CV, not decorate it.

Photos

People often include photos of themselves on their CV. Don't! Unless you are applying to be a model or to work as an actor/actress, then including a photo with/on your CV is definitely not recommended.

The whole point of a CV is that recruiters have a brief, factual description of your abilities, and photographs often allow them, rightly or wrongly, to develop a preconceived idea of you as a person and this might well count against you. They may have an irrational aversion to facial hair, for example! An interview is the most appropriate place for the recruiter to first see an applicant, not the CV.

Even if you do have movie star looks (and I don't think many of us do; personally I look nothing like Brad Pitt), it isn't a good idea. People *will* discriminate whether there are laws in place to ban them from doing so or not. This is a point which often confuses many of our foreign clients because it is still perfectly normal in Europe and elsewhere to include a photo, but definitely not in the UK.

If you must include a photograph (and some recruiters/employers will insist on it, even though it comes very close to flouting anti-discrimination legislation), then make sure it is an appropriately professional passport-style photograph.

There are those who point out that a picture speaks a thousand words and that the use of photography is vitally important in marketing.

Yes, photography is extremely important in marketing and advertising. Yes, your CV is a marketing document which advertises you to prospective employers. But it is not accepted practice in the UK to include a photograph, and whilst it's often great to stand out from the crowd, this is decidedly not a method that is recommended.

If you're sending your CV by email then the inclusion of a photo can also cause problems with anti-virus software. Your CV could be automatically deleted!

Exceptions to the rules

There aren't many exceptions to the rules I've laid out in this chapter. If you work within a highly creative and artistic field, then you may be able to bend or even break some of the rules. I'll cover this in Chapter 16: Special cases – professions where the rules are different.

Emailing your application

You probably have a number of questions on your mind about emailing applications and I will try to answer all of these here.

Generally speaking, there's not too much difference between sending an application by post and sending an application by email.

➤ You still need to make an impact.

➤ You're still competing against countless others for the reader's attention.

➤ You still need to give them a compelling reason to read your CV (except that in this case they won't have it right there in front of them; they need to open it separately).

There are, however, certain practicalities you need to deal with.

Subject line: never leave it blank! It's extremely unprofessional to do so. Keep it short and simple. You could specify the vacancy title and reference if applicable. If you're making a speculative application then you might need to be a little more inventive and make a greater effort to catch the recipient's attention. Don't go over the top, though; you certainly don't want to risk your email being labelled as spam and discarded.

Form of address: just because this is an email is no reason to start with 'Hi' or suchlike. Start your email just as you would start a professional letter. This isn't an email to a pal; it's an important job application.

Content: I would definitely not recommend sending both your CV and cover letter as email attachments. The chances of either of them getting read will drop dramatically. I believe CVs should always be sent as attachments (because they normally look awful when copied and pasted into an email), but you should place the contents of your cover letter in the body of your email. (The exception to this is when a recruiter has specifically requested 'no attachments'.) By including any kind of attachment with your email you run the risk of falling foul of spam filters. Anti-spam software is becoming increasingly sophisticated; consequently, people are becoming less paranoid about attachments they receive; not so long ago many companies had a policy of deleting all emails with attachments!

Signature: many people have an automated email signature, which goes out at the bottom of every email they send. Whatever yours says, remember that it will be seen by potential employers. You might decide a rewrite is in order!

Filenames: don't just call your CV 'CV'. Make sure it contains your name, e.g. 'Jane Bloggs – CV'. Organisations receive many files simply called 'CV'. It's easy for confusions to arise.

File format: Microsoft Word is the most universally accepted format for a document (apart from 'plain text', which is not very attractive). If you send your CV in a different format then you're immediately reducing the chances of the recipient being able to access it (unless you work in a creative field, e.g. a graphic designer). Do you think the recipient will write politely back and ask for your CV in a different format? Or do you think it's more likely they will probably just delete your email?

Cc and Bcc: when your application needs to be sent to more than one individual, you will need to use the Cc function and possibly the Bcc function. Never use these functions to spam multiple employers with exactly the same email. Each application you make should be tailored for the organisation to which you are sending it.

BLOOPER!

Be careful with files and filenames. I received a file from a job applicant titled 'CV', which simply said:

What's at the bottom of my garden

Spider

Worm

Beetle

Bug

Needless to say, he didn't get the job.

Chapter **3**

Content and style:
what to say
and how to say it

It is extremely important to phrase information in such a way as to sell yourself as effectively as possible.

Your CV is your personal sales brochure and needs to be written accordingly.

It is also important to strike the right balance between too little and too much text. To achieve this, you need to be very careful how you phrase the content.

Person, pronouns and verbs

There's a lot of confusion about the 'person' in which you should write your CV.

If you're not sure what a 'grammatical person' is then allow me to explain.

In English, we have three grammatical persons, each of which is denoted by different personal pronouns.

➤ *'I' and 'we' denote the first person.*

➤ *'You' denotes the second person (both singular and plural).*

➤ *'He', 'she', 'it' and 'they' denote the third person.*

The verb which follows these personal pronouns will often take a different form dependent on the person involved (and whether it is singular or plural). One of the most common examples is the verb 'to be'.

➤ *I am*

➤ *You are*

➤ *He is*

Most verbs vary in one way or another depending on the tense. Take the verb 'to possess' as an example.

➤ *I possess.*

➤ *You possess.*

➤ *He possesses.*

To make life even more complicated, these pronouns come in a variety of different forms. Those mentioned above are 'nominative' (or 'subjective') pronouns. There are also accusative (or 'objective'), genitive (or 'possessive') and even reflexive forms.

➤ *For the first person these are me, my/mine and myself.*

➤ *For the third-person masculine they are him, his and himself.*

➤ *For the third-person feminine they are her, her/hers and herself.*

Some schools of thought say that a CV should be written in the first person; others will say it should be written in the third person. The problem is that the individuals behind these different opinions often don't really understand what they're talking about! The terms 'first person' and 'third person' are frequently misunderstood.

You will have to choose either the first person or the third person when writing your CV. It's one or the other. My recommendation would be to use the third person, not the first person.

The words 'I' and 'me' are often used repeatedly in homemade CVs. Making a CV too personal by writing in the first person:

➤ *can make it hard not to sound arrogant or egocentric;*

➤ *tends to come across as rather unprofessional; and*

➤ *is simply too informal for the circumstances.*

'I this ...', 'I that ...', 'I the other ...', 'me, me, me!' This is not the impression you want to give the reader.

It might seem unnatural to write a document about you and never use either I or me but recruitment experts generally agree that this is the best way to do it. Don't give your reader I-strain!

The third person can sound a little stuffy at times but it generally reads better and comes across as more professional. It gives you greater scope to brag about yourself without actually sounding as if you're bragging!

I'm certainly not saying you should litter your CV with 'he', 'she', 'his', 'her' etc. either.

The best solution is to use the third person and keep your use of all pronouns to a minimum. They're simply not necessary as every reader will know that *your* CV is a document about *you*.

Let's take a simple statement written in the first person as an example:

I possess excellent interpersonal, communication and negotiation skills. I am able to work well on my own initiative and I can demonstrate the levels of self-motivation needed to meet my tightest deadlines.

If you convert this to the third person and strip out the pronouns you get:

Possesses excellent interpersonal, communication and negotiation skills. Able to work well on own initiative and can demonstrate the levels of self-motivation needed to meet the tightest of deadlines.

This is the style in which you should be aiming to write your CV.

As always with CVs, there is no rule which applies 100 per cent of the time and if you really struggle to word it in the third person, then you can use the first person for your *Professional* profile and for your *Objective*. But you should categorically stick to the third person for your *Career history*.

Action verbs

We've covered how to use verbs. Now let's address which verbs you should be using.

An effective way of making your CV have a greater impact is to start your sentences with what are commonly known as 'action verbs'. These are words such as:

➤ Achieved
➤ Accomplished
➤ Developed
➤ Launched
➤ Managed
➤ Maximised
➤ Strengthened
➤ Improved
➤ Implemented
➤ Realised

I have included a comprehensive list in Appendix A: 250 action verbs just in case you are struggling to find exactly the right word for your particular circumstances.

These words can be used to describe your skills and experiences in such a way as to emphasise what you achieved rather than just what you did.

Choose your action verbs carefully so they are as relevant as possible to the role for which you are applying.

The words in my list are all in the past tense. You can easily convert them to the present tense if you're writing about your current job, e.g. 'developed' becomes 'develops'. However, this can make for awkward reading. Your best bet is to use what is known as the present participle, e.g. 'developing'.

Positive adjectives

You will also want to use a good spread of positive adjectives to help reinforce your statements. Here are some examples:

➤ Consistent
➤ Efficient
➤ Experienced
➤ Innovative
➤ Positive
➤ Productive
➤ Proficient
➤ Resourceful
➤ Successful
➤ Versatile

And I have included a comprehensive list in Appendix B: 50 positive adjectives.

Accompanying adverbs

Many of these positive adjectives can be converted to adverbs where necessary, e.g. 'successful' becomes 'successfully', 'consistent' becomes 'consistently' etc.

Avoiding repetition

Although it can be difficult, you should try hard to avoid repetition in your CV.

This is especially the case with the starting words of bullet points, e.g. developed, implemented, because this always stands out more to the eye than other repetition. Within any one list of bullet points, try to start each bullet point with a different word. Within any one paragraph, avoid using the same adjective, adverb or action verb twice.

Jargon

Feel free to highlight your knowledge and understanding of your work by using relevant terminology and 'buzzwords' but this should not be overdone.

Excessive jargon is not recommended, particularly since CVs may initially be reviewed by a central HR (human resources) department whose staff may quite simply not understand a lot of the jargon specific to your role.

TOP TIP

If you need to use a specialist/technical term that you are not sure the reader will understand, then it is perfectly acceptable to follow it with a brief definition in brackets. Be careful not to insult the reader's intelligence.

Numbers

Numbers often create more of an impact than words. If you really want to maximise the impact, you should aim to qualify your statements with specific figures wherever possible. Using qualifying adjectives such as 'major', 'substantial' and 'significant' is all very well but try to quote precise figures and percentages if at all possible. Don't just make a claim back up that claim.

For example, you could say:

Directly responsible for supervising a regional team of sales executives

However, it's always going to be more impressive to say:

Directly responsible for supervising a regional team of 24 sales executives

Always quantify where possible, whether it's simple figures, percentages or pound notes:

Led the introduction of a major culture change in customer service, improving customer satisfaction ratings from 6.2 out of 10 to 8.3 out of 10

Personally responsible for delivering the highest sales contribution for the group of 24.4%, with the closest rival delivering just 15.8%

Successfully tendering for a £2.3 million refurbishment project with a healthy 15% profit margin

Publishing convention often dictates that the numbers one to ten be written out in full in text, whereas figures should be used for any number higher than that. For example, you can say 314 but you have to spell out seven. This convention is fine for general publishing and is commonly observed in books, magazines and newspapers. However, your CV is not a normal piece of writing; it is a marketing document, and in marketing the normal rules don't necessarily apply. I would recommend quoting all numbers in figures rather than letters because they're a lot more eye-catching that way and are likely to achieve a greater impact.

Percentages: it is also a common publishing convention for the symbol % to be written as 'per cent'. Again, I would advise against this for the same reasons, additionally, a % symbol takes up less space and has greater visual impact.

Money, money, money: when it comes to specifying quantities of money, it is accepted practice to abbreviate thousands to the letter k, e.g. £45,000 to £45k. Millions can be similarly abbreviated, e.g. £2.3m, but this is less common and the full word million has more of a psychological impact.

Spelling, typos and punctuation

STATISTIC

Sixty per cent of CVs and cover letters contain at least one linguistic error.

For documents which are supposed to be perfect that's a fairly staggering proportion, isn't it?

It is impossible to stress enough how important this issue is. Spelling and grammatical errors are amongst the most irritating errors a recruiter sees, amongst the most damaging errors you can make and are also amongst the most easily avoided. The answer is to check, check and check again, and then have someone else check for good measure!

Reading through your CV yourself is essential; having a friend or colleague read through it is even better because it's easy to miss mistakes in your own work when you've been staring at it for hours.

Spelling

Spelling errors can make a huge difference to your career prospects.

In one unfortunate case, an individual got very confused about the difference between 'role' and 'roll'. He kept referring, throughout both his CV and his cover letter, to the various 'rolls' he had had, such as 'an important roll in the finance department' and 'sharing a roll with another colleague'.

BLOOPER!

Another interesting example was the receptionist who spent all day receiving and transmitting massages!

Commonly misspelled words

Any word can be misspelled, even mispelled! However, some words are frequently misspelled in CVs and these are the ones you should keep a particularly careful eye out for:

➤ Separate – often seen spelled as seperate

➤ Necessary – neccesary, necessery, nesessary

➤ Liaising – most commonly misspelled as liasing

➤ Liaison – likewise misspelled as liason

➤ Personnel – personnell, personell, personel

And I have included a comprehensive list in Appendix C: 222 commonly misspelled words.

Easily confused words

There are also various pairs of words which I commonly see used incorrectly in CVs and cover letters that I'd like to draw to your attention. It can be a little complicated, so if you get confused I suggest you get out the dictionary!

➤ principle/principal

'The principal problem you might face with a new project is that you don't agree, in principle, with the approach the management wants you to take.'

'Principle' is a noun, commonly referring to a personal belief or conviction, e.g. 'It's against my principles.' Alternatively, it can refer to how something works, e.g. 'The principle of a hot air balloon is very simple.'

'Principal', however, can be both an adjective and a noun. As an adjective, it normally means first, main or chief, e.g. 'My principal objection is the cost.' As a noun, however, it has a whole host of different meanings.

➤ stationery/stationary

'You might be responsible for ordering stationery supplies from the stationer. However, if you're stuck in your car at the traffic lights then you're stationary!'

'Stationery' is a noun for writing materials such as paper and pens. 'Stationary' is an adjective, which means not moving or standing still.

➤ complement/compliment

'If you and a colleague successfully complete a project together then you should pay each other a compliment for a job well done. Alternatively, if he possesses certain skills that you don't, or vice versa, then you might say that you complement each other.'

The two words have very different meanings.

➤ arise/arouse

'A rude and abusive call centre worker could easily cause customer complaints to arise, which might arouse a rather angry response from the management.'

BLOOPER!

....

'Swiftly and effectively resolving any customer complaints which might arouse.'

➤ effect/affect

'You can effect a change, and depending on the circumstances, you can also affect a change. However, whilst a change will have an effect it can't have an affect. And whilst you might be affected by a change you certainly can't be effected by it.'

This is a complicated one!

➤ advice/advise

'You might advise your clients not to sue the local newspaper but they might decide to totally ignore your advice.'

'Advice' is a noun and 'advise' is a verb. They're not only different words; they're also pronounced differently.

➤ practice/practise

'You can work in a doctor's practice and you can put your ideas into practice, but if you want to deliver an outstanding presentation to a potential client then you had better practise!'

Whilst pronounced the same, practice is a noun and practise is a verb.

In American English, the word 'practise' doesn't actually exist at all. Americans use practice both as a noun and a verb and this is just one of many differences between British English and American English.

Let's take a closer look at the vagaries of our American cousins.

Across the pond ...

The differences between British English and American English are numerous and often cause confusion.

The bottom line is that if you're looking for work in the UK you should be using British English spelling.

We've covered 'practice'/'practise'. Here's another problematic pair:

➤ licence/license

'Licence' is a noun in British English and 'license' is a verb. A driving examiner can license you to drive but the plastic card you'll get is your licence. Americans, on the other hand, don't use the word 'licence' at all. They use license both as a noun and as a verb.

A particular problem is that word-processing software (for example, Microsoft Word) is often set to American spelling by default rather than British English (because the software creators are normally American). It will therefore highlight some words as incorrect even when they're not; they're just British English spellings and not American spellings. This can be resolved by ensuring that the document is set to UK spelling.

TOP TIP

In Microsoft Word 2013:

- ➤ click on the 'File' tab
- ➤ click 'Options'
- ➤ click 'Language'
- ➤ in the 'Choose Editing Languages' section 'Add' 'English (United Kingdom)'
- ➤ 'Remove' 'English (United States)'
- ➤ 'Set as Default' 'English (United Kingdom)'
- ➤ close all your Office 2013 programs and then open them again for the change to take effect

For other word-processing packages you can consult the user guide or use the built-in help facility. Failing that, you can find the solution online.

Fully capitalised words

Fully capitalised words are also a problem because spell checks commonly ignore these. This is, again, only the default setting and can be changed.

TOP TIP

In Microsoft Word 2013:

- ➤ Click on the 'File' tab
- ➤ Click 'Options'
- ➤ Click 'Proofing'
- ➤ Uncheck the box next to 'Ignore words in UPPERCASE'

You also need to be careful with acronyms, e.g. BBC, IEEE, CPID, FTP.

Typos

Typos or typographical errors can be harder to spot than plain spelling errors. A spell check won't pick up on mistakes such as 'working in a busty office'! You may be surprised, but this sort of error is not unusual. Take a look at where the letters t and y sit on a keyboard; right next to each other. It's very easy to try to hit the y and get a ty instead.

Another common typo is to completely miss out a letter: 'worked closely with the Finance Manger'.

BLOOPER!

I've certainly seen some interesting job titles. I had one client who was a metal health advisor and another who was looking for work as a diary farmer!

It is essential to run a spell check through the finished CV as well as carefully proofread it.

And it's not just words, it can be numbers too:

1881–1995: BA (Hons) English Literature

That's a very long time to be a student!

Superfluous spaces

You should also be careful to eliminate all superfluous spaces between words, for example 'eliminate superfluous spaces' has two spaces between 'eliminate' and 'superfluous'.

Word-processing software will often help you by highlighting such errors, depending on what type and settings you've got (often with green underlining).

Freudian slips

A final type of spelling/typing error I'd like to cover is where the writer picks the wrong word.

These can be of the banal sort where you type 'their' instead of 'there' or 'your' instead of 'you're'. You know which is correct but your brain somehow sends a different message to the keyboard.

Alternatively, typos can be rather more interesting! One which immediately springs to my mind is the hopeful jobseeker who stated she was 'a conscious employee'. You'd hope so, really.

BLOOPER!

Probably one of the best typos I've seen was by a candidate explaining that he was 'financially incompetent'!

You probably think I'm making all of this up but, trust me it wouldn't be in this book if I hadn't actually seen it!

A spell check won't detect these problems but a prospective employer very possibly will.

Again, careful proofreading is the answer.

Punctuation

Errors in punctuation are the most common grammatical errors, and the apostrophe is definitely the most abused. For example:

Londons' No. 1 retailer of kitchen appliances

Or, possibly even worse:

Londons No. 1 retailer of kitchen appliances

The correct usage is:

London's No. 1 retailer of kitchen appliances

If you're not sure what the rules are then there are plenty of articles on the Internet which explain correct punctuation in detail.

'It's' and 'its' are also frequently misused. And you sometimes even see *its'*, which doesn't exist at all!

'It's' is a contraction of 'it is' or 'it has', whereas 'its' is a possessive pronoun, e.g. 'When it's necessary, the computer will automatically update its anti-virus software.'

Poor old apostrophes – so frequently mistreated. The plural of CV isn't CV's. It is CVs. However, even some of The CV Centre®'s competitors get this wrong on their websites!

BLOOPER!

I was amazed the other day to see a headline in the *Daily Mail* saying: 'Greek tragedy means its boom time in Belgravia.' It seems this is an issue that even professional journalists have difficulty with.

It's not always black and white, of course. Whilst it is grammatically correct to say 'four years' experience', we find a lot of our clients initially complain when we do this, thinking it's an error! Many people assume it should be 'four year's experience'. You might fear (and reasonably so) that a recruiter may also think it is a mistake and so it is better for you to make a deliberate error. The choice is yours. This is the only time I would ever consider recommending anything less than grammatical perfection!

Open and closed punctuation

You will (or certainly should) be using a lot of bullet points in your CV, so I'd like to clarify an important punctuation issue specific to bullet points.

Bullet points do not need full stops at the end ('closed' punctuation) unless they are actual grammatically correct sentences (which they generally won't be).

➤ This is a bullet point.

This is obviously a full sentence and so ends with a full stop.
However, most bullet points will read along the lines of:

➤ Successfully implementing new procedures leading to a capacity increase exceeding 30%

This is not a full sentence and so doesn't need a full stop at the end.
Can you spot any spelling, grammatical or typographical errors in this book? We hope not! But if you do, then please visit **www.jamesinn.es** to let us know so we can correct them in the next edition.

Can I leave things out of my CV?

This is a common question I get asked and the answer is not only can you leave things out of your CV, there are certain things you *should* leave out of your CV.

One incongruity I remember concerns a client who was a banking executive with a PhD, who insisted on both his O levels (plus grades) and information regarding his captaincy of the school cricket team (quite a few decades ago) being included.

He was clearly an extreme case, but most of the CVs I see contain unnecessary clutter in one form or another.

Look at each piece of information which could be included in your CV and ask yourself, 'Does this help to support my case?' If it doesn't then leave it out. You are under no obligation to include everything in your CV.

In most instances you can eliminate what a prospective employer might see as unnecessary detail; for example, list only years, not months, within your *Career history*, which also helps to cover up any chronological gaps. (Medical professions are an exception.)

Concentrate on your recent history and summarise older information. If you've got A levels then don't list all your GCSEs/O levels. Similarly, if you've got a degree, there's generally no need to include A-level grades unless there's a particular reason to do so, e.g. they're all A or B grades. Employers are most interested in what you've done most recently, although they generally still need to know the basics of older information.

The truth, the whole truth ...

A large percentage of people seem to think it's permissible to tell a few small porkies when writing their CV. Many think it's acceptable because 'everyone else does it', and it is a fact that many prospective employers do not check an applicant's information as thoroughly as they perhaps should. However, I would always strongly caution everyone against telling anything but the truth on their CV.

Besides the moral aspect, any inaccuracies on a CV can give an employer grounds to dismiss an employee immediately for gross misconduct, – and employers do have ways of checking up on you.

You could even become unstuck during the interview, before you even get offered the job. One candidate claimed to be fluent in French on his CV and then got quite a shock when he came up against a half-French/half-English interviewer who thought it quite reasonable to conduct the interview in French!

And it's not going to do your interview nerves much good worrying about whether or not you are going to be unmasked as a liar. This is a surprisingly common cause of pre-interview jitters.

But doesn't everyone do it?

STATISTIC

∙∙

Surveys show that between 20 per cent and 35 per cent of candidates lie to one degree or another when it comes to writing their CV.

It all depends on how you define 'lie'. Twenty per cent engage in a 'significant' lie (the kind where you could be sacked for gross misconduct as a result), whereas up to 35 per cent include at least one small porky here or there.

But just because 'everyone else does it' it doesn't mean that you should. Not everyone lies on their CV – it remains a minority and it is very questionable whether those that do lie gain any benefit from it.

Whether or not you tell the whole truth is another matter entirely. You are under no obligation to include every detail of your life history in your

CV and any information which could be perceived negatively should be omitted or excluded. Examples include being fired from a previous job.

You should always put as positive a spin as possible on the contents of your CV but it's a fine line and only you can be the judge of what is and is not acceptable.

I once read a CV which proudly declared the candidate had worked as a 'Freelance importer', importing 'various types of merchandise into Jordan – exotic animals, motorbikes, guns etc.'

Mentioning that you imported arms into the Middle East is unlikely to be well received by the reader, unless of course that is the line of business you are in. (Incidentally, in this particular case, the candidate was applying for work as an office manager.)

Graduates seem to be particularly prone to inaccuracies on their CVs; the worst error is deliberately falsifying the class of their university degree.

Deliberately falsifying your degree class is definitely not recommended. However, you can of course simply be economical with the truth, e.g. only list your degree class if it is a 1st or a 2:1.

Chapter **4**

Structure: which type of CV is right for you?

In the previous couple of chapters I have covered general principles which could apply to almost anybody setting out to write a CV. Now we need to make a decision as to what specific structure of CV you should use. Readers of this book will range from school leavers right the way up to senior executives, so the way you structure your CV will depend very much on your own personal circumstances.

First of all, let me define what are generally seen as the two main types of CV structure that you can use.

Chronological and functional CVs

The two main CV types are: chronological (or reverse chronological, to be precise) and functional.

The chronological CV lists your employment (and academic) history beginning with the most recent and working backwards, with a brief description under each position. This is by far the most widely used.

The functional CV lists your experience under different functional areas, such as marketing or customer service, and this forms the main core of the CV. It focuses on specific skills rather than a full history (making it appropriate for those with a very varied career history). It will include a *Key skills* section and it will use a *Career summary* instead of a full *Career history*.

The mixed CV

Between them, these two principal types give rise to a third type, known as the mixed or hybrid CV. A hybrid CV is quite a mix of the chronological and functional types. It lists skills/experience under different functions at the top of the CV and then goes on to list previous positions in reverse chronological order.

Other CV types

You may have heard other terms such as an 'inventory CV' and 'targeted CV' but these are not in common use. It is best to focus on the three types I described above.

Which to use?

The question I really want to answer is which style of CV will generate the most interviews.

STATISTIC

We have conducted careful surveys of our clients and our findings clearly demonstrate that functional CVs do not work as well as chronological CVs in terms of winning interviews, at least not in the majority of cases. If they don't get interviews then they shouldn't be used; it's as simple as that.

Recruiters will often bin functional CVs, as they need to see exactly what the candidate has done and where to really ascertain if they are suitable for the vacancy. There is also the tendency to think that those sending a functional CV are trying to bury or hide something, or want the recruiter to think that they have more experience than they actually do have.

Not all recruiters are the same, of course, but the majority aren't particularly fond of the functional CV. Job hunting being a numbers game, it consequently pays to cater to the majority view. However, you should be aware that some recruiters, having received a chronological CV, will then want to see a functional CV as well especially for senior executive positions.

And not all candidates are the same either. Individuals for whom a functional CV might be more appropriate include those with very little practical work experience, those seeking to move out of one line of work and into another; for example, from military life to civilian life, or those whose professions cause them to change job/contract particularly frequently. We'll cover various special cases such as these in Chapter 15: Ten solutions for ten potential problems, and Chapter 16: Special cases – professions where the rules are different.

The mixed type can also be appropriate for certain cases. Many of you may see it as offering the best of both worlds and it is an increasingly popular structure to use.

Section order

Another key structural decision to make is whether to list your *Education and qualifications* before your *Career history* or vice versa.

It all depends on what is your greater selling point. You should make sure that all your most important information is conveyed on the first page, or for a one-page CV, in the top half of the page.

Which do you feel is more likely to be of interest to a prospective employer, your *Education and qualifications* or your *Career history*?

If you've just graduated and have little work experience then the *Education and qualifications* section is going to be of much greater interest. However, if you left school 40 years ago then it is obviously your *Career history* which is going to be more important to a recruiter.

Even if you have only a little work experience and are only qualified to GCSE level you may feel that your *Career history* is the greater selling point and that you should lead with that rather than your *Education and qualifications*. It's your call. It's all about conveying the most important, most relevant and most powerful information first.

Depending on your circumstances you may have a whole range of additional sections to include within your CV, for instance, *Publications, and Research*. Again, you'll need to give careful thought to the order in which you present them. Order them logically and according to the value they contribute.

Reverse chronological order

It is a standard convention on CVs to use reverse chronological order, i.e. to present your most recent information first, followed by older and, consequently, less relevant information. I would strongly suggest you make sure your CV conforms to this.

Many people find this illogical and don't feel comfortable with the idea. But look at it this way: should the first job you ever had be the first thing a prospective employer sees when looking at your *Career history*? If you're now a managing director, then your first job is probably going to look a tad irrelevant. And when they look at your *Education and qualifications* what should they read first, details of the GCSEs you sat ten years ago? Or details of the MA in Applied Communication that you've just completed?

It's obvious, isn't it?

TOP TIP

. . . .

CVs should always be written in reverse chronological order with the most recent and, therefore, most important items within a section coming first.

Reverse chronological order applies only to the individual entries under each section, not to the order of the sections. We've already established that whether you should lead with *Education and qualifications* or whether you should lead with *Career history* depends on various different factors. The basic principle is the same; it's all about conveying the most important, most relevant and most powerful information first.

Length

I have seen CVs over 30 pages long (true!) with photocopies of all the individuals' certificates on top of that.

This is not an autobiography you're writing. It's a curriculum vitae. It's a lot shorter!

I always advocate a one-page CV if it is feasible; some recruitment agencies, especially head-hunters, may insist on a one-page CV.

Failing that, two pages are entirely acceptable, and in certain circumstances it may be acceptable for a CV to run to three or more pages, but only for certain special cases, such as medical and engineering professions. These are the exceptions that prove the rule, and we'll be covering them in greater detail later in the book under Chapter 16: Special cases – professions where the rules are different.

People often feel that a one-page CV is worth less than a two-pager, but this is definitely not true. It is much better to have a good strong one-page CV than a two-page one that is padded out with unnecessary information. You should always be aiming to exclude irrelevant information which may detract from other more important points.

Often a CV which has been spread out over two pages can, with a little careful tweaking, be made to fit onto one page and this tends to have greater impact. It is important not to force a CV onto one page when two pages would be better; a one-page CV tends to look incomplete and weak.

Regardless of the length, as I said previously, make sure that all your most important information is conveyed on the first page of a multi-page CV or in the top half of a one-page CV because many recruiters simply won't bother to look any further.

What if your finished CV is more than two pages long?

There's only one answer to this question; unless yours is a special case, you need to keep working on your CV until you've reduced it to the standard two pages.

Take a long hard look at your CV and consider:

➤ Removing some of the less important points you've made

➤ Finding ways to communicate the same points more concisely

➤ Ruthlessly eliminating all unnecessary words and phrases

➤ Axing non-essential sections, for example, your *Objective*

➤ Placing your *Interests and activities* under *Other details*

➤ Changing the design and page layout to create more space

➤ Editing, rewriting, polishing and perfecting until it fits!

PART 2

BUILDING YOUR CV: SECTION BY SECTION

Chapter **5**

Personal details

We've discussed the general principles of aesthetics, presentation and content and established which type of CV is most appropriate for you.

Building on that, this and the following chapters will take each of the principal sections you may include in your CV and discuss each one in detail showing you how to configure each section to give you a real winning advantage.

So let's get going.

Personal details

It is vital that the reader can spot, at a glance, your name and precisely how to get in contact with you.

Your CV should be headed boldly and clearly with your name followed by your contact details. It should not be headed 'Curriculum Vitae' or 'CV' or anything else.

Just your name. And only your first name and your last name.

Traditionally, CVs were headed with 'Curriculum Vitae' or suchlike, but this convention is very much on the way out, which is probably a good thing given how frequently it is misspelled!

BLOOPER!

One candidate headed his CV 'Kuriculam Vitay'!

Problematic names

I regularly attend recruitment events promoting diversity in the workplace, events which are attended by a high proportion of individuals of different ethnic origins, and I am often asked:

➤ What if your name is difficult for the average English speaker to pronounce?

➤ Do you have to state your 'official' name, i.e. as on your passport?

➤ If you're known by a shortened version of your name, is it acceptable to use that?

My answer to these questions is that you can – within the limits of common sense – call yourself more or less what you like on your CV. There are no legal restrictions provided you're not attempting to defraud. If you use an alternative, abbreviated or anglicised first name on a regular basis then there's no reason why you can't also use it on your CV. Changing your last name to a shortened version is equally acceptable. The key issue is not to hide your real identity from a prospective employer. When the time comes to deal with contracts of employment you should make them fully aware of your full official name.

Another popular question is, 'What if it's not obvious from my first name what my gender is?'

The answer's simple. You can include your title (Mr, Mrs etc.) on your CV before your first name. There is certainly no harm in this if it is necessary to clarify your gender. You can also do the same on any cover letters you write.

Your key contact details

You should follow your name with your key contact details. How to present these details? It's much more aesthetically pleasing (and looks a lot more professional) to present these as a letterhead, rather than in a list like a form. It also saves a lot of valuable space.

Head the CV with your name and follow it with your address and other contact details, including your phone numbers and email address. Place your address on one line with your phone numbers on the next and finish with your email address.

Addresses

It is generally unnecessary to include UK county names in an address. Royal Mail–approved addressing never uses county names. It can be useful, however, if you are applying for work a long way from where you currently live (if, for example, you are planning to relocate) and you feel that the organisations to which you are applying probably won't be able to work out where you are currently living from the name of your nearest town alone.

It should be noted that there is no need for a comma between city names and postcodes.

Telephone numbers

Phone numbers should always include the local area code. The correct spacing (according to British Telecom) for London, Belfast etc. is 020 7946 0000. For elsewhere it's 01632 960 960. This separates the code out and makes the remainder easier to read.

If you are stating more than one phone number then it's a good idea to specify what each number is; for example, 'Tel: 01632 960 960 (home); 07700 900 900 (mobile)'. If you're only including one number then there's no need.

If you're based in one country and your prospective employer is based in another country, then you should endeavour to include international dialling codes with your phone numbers.

I would suggest you avoid using a work telephone number. Even if the current employer knows you are looking elsewhere and is happy for you to use your work telephone number for this purpose, your prospective employer doesn't know this and might think it indicates a lack of respect. A mobile number is much better. It also gives any interested parties one single number on which they can reach you 24 hours a day, seven days a week.

Email addresses

Whilst not having an email address at all on your CV is clearly a problem, it's not something I see very often. Far more common is the use of fun or jokey email addresses.

Whilst these may be fine for corresponding with friends and family, employers will probably regard more serious email addresses as simply more professional.

Many recruiters report seeing inappropriate email addresses on CVs and this doesn't do the candidates any favours. Think about what your email address says about you. Email addresses such as sexylady@ example.com and hunkyjoe@example.com, or getting really risqué here, mistressdominatrix@example.com and wickedandwild@example.com, will clearly not help you to present a professional image. (By the way, I haven't completely invented these email addresses; I have adapted them from real email addresses I've seen on CVs and have just changed them slightly to protect the innocent! Or not so innocent!)

You might have the perfect CV, but if your email address is mrluvverman@example.com then it may harm your chances. I would suggest you open a new email account to use for professional purposes (e.g. Hotmail or Yahoo!) and keep your professional correspondence separate from your personal correspondence.

Convention dictates that email addresses should not be capitalised. Aesthetically it's probably more attractive to keep them in lowercase.

I'd also like to add that you should make sure that your email address doesn't appear as a hyperlink in your CV, i.e. in blue underlined text.

Whilst this could arguably be useful in certain circumstances, it can also mean that the email address doesn't print properly to a black-and-white printer, which is a significant problem. In Microsoft Office you can remove a hyperlink by simply right-clicking on it and selecting 'Remove Hyperlink' from the menu that pops up.

Finally, I would suggest you avoid using a work email address for the same reasons that you should avoid using a work telephone number. And if your current employer doesn't know you are looking elsewhere then don't forget that they are legally permitted to monitor all of your use of their computer facilities. They're not paying you to hunt for another job!

Case study

Jane's personal email address is jumpingjane@example.com, so she decides it would be best to open a new email account just for her professional correspondence: janebloggs@example.com. Her finished letterhead looks like this:

Jane Bloggs

1 Any Road, Anytown AN1 1CV
Telephone: 01632 960 960 (home); 07700 900 900 (mobile)
Email: janebloggs@example.com

Date of birth

I often get asked whether or not you should include your date of birth (or age) on a CV. The old answer to this used to be that you should include it because recruiters expect to see it and so if you don't include it then it'll just draw attention to the fact that it has been omitted.

However, with the introduction of the Employment Equality (Age) Regulations 2006 (now superseded by the Equality Act 2010) this is no longer the case. And, besides, any recruiter worth his or her salt will be able to deduce pretty accurately exactly how old you are just by looking at your education, qualifications and experience.

There is also a security (identity fraud) risk involved in volunteering this sort of highly personal data to all and sundry. Should your CV fall into the wrong hands, this is precisely the sort of information an identity fraudster needs to clone your identity.

Marital status: Single. Unmarried. Unengaged. Uninvolved. No commitments.

Yes, one individual really did put the above on his CV!

My clients often feel that it is compulsory to include details such as their marital status, nationality, number (and ages) of children/dependants etc. Whilst, yes, it certainly used to be the norm to include this sort of information on a CV, it is now increasingly rare, given modern anti-discrimination legislation, to find these details on a CV. They simply aren't relevant.

Too many candidates get too personal. A recruiter does not need to know whether or not you're married, how many children you have, where you like to go on holiday, what your partner's name is, what you normally have for breakfast.... These facts should not affect whether or not you can do the job! They simply clutter up your CV, making it harder for the recruiters to get to the key information that they really need to see.

I have seen a whole range of irrelevant personal information on CVs: maiden name, partner's occupation, even religious belief. I've seen CVs that include totally superfluous details such as National Insurance number, passport number and place of birth. Yes, your employer will eventually need to know your National Insurance number but not at this early stage. And they should never need to know your place of birth.

BLOOPER!

Other more extreme cases I have seen include candidates detailing their:

➤ Height – I am 6 foot 5 inches tall.
➤ Weight – I weigh 18 stone.
➤ Shoe size – I take a size 10 shoe.
➤ Complexion – Fair (wheatish).

The only circumstances in which you would need to provide this sort of information is if you're in acting or modelling. (Needless to say, none of the individuals who put the details above on their CVs was in any way connected to acting or modelling.)

One lovey-dovey young couple looking for work as live-in domestic help went so far as to proclaim on their CVs that they had to work together because they were 'inseparable soulmates: old souls reunited again from a distant past' (probably late 1960s Haight-Ashbury!). They went on to express their 'love of children'. Would you let people like that anywhere near your offspring?!

Identity fraud

Besides being entirely superfluous to the recruitment process, including certain personal details will expose you to an increased risk of identity fraud.

STATISTIC

Fifty per cent of all CVs contain sufficient quantity of personal data to enable an identity fraudster to successfully apply for a credit card.

The most useful information to a fraudster is your name and full postal address in conjunction with your date of birth. Marital status is also very useful.

Many people seem determined to include all sorts of other information on their CV, most of which is really only of use to a fraudster; for example, place of birth and passport number. Each piece of information is fairly harmless on its own, but collectively they provide a perfect opportunity for a fraudster to clone and abuse your identity.

Too few people realise the potential consequences if the personal information contained within their CV were to fall into the wrong hands.

Chapter **6**

Professional profile

So, what exactly is a *Professional profile*?

You've probably heard of the term but you may well be unsure as to what it really means.

A *Professional profile* is a brief statement at the beginning of a CV, which, in the space of a few short lines, conveys your key personal and professional characteristics. It's essentially an introduction to your CV and should give the reader a compelling overview before they read on in further detail.

Other terms you may have heard include *Personal profile* and *Career profile*. The former concentrates more on personal characteristics and the latter on your career and work experience. A well-written *Professional profile* successfully combines the two.

Should you include a *Professional profile* on your CV?

There are some people who argue that professional profiles should not be included on CVs anymore because they can come across as being too self-centred and pompous. However, the majority of recruiters and employers remain in favour of them; I almost always advocate the inclusion of a *Professional profile* within a CV.

Some people wonder why a CV needs to have a *Professional profile* if you have included a similar summary within your cover letter. The answer is simply that the person conducting an interview may not necessarily see the cover letter. It is not uncommon for whoever does the initial sift of CVs to remove them. And organisations using scanning software will often only scan in CVs, not cover letters.

The *Professional profile* can be used to effectively summarise your skills and attributes that you will expound in the main body of the CV and they are also very useful for CVs that are specifically targeted towards a certain position, as they can be used to emphasise the essential criteria that you are able to fulfil. It is a key area to tailor for different applications.

A final reason for creating a *Professional profile* is that the No. 1 question you are likely to be asked at interview is, 'Can you tell me a bit about yourself?' This is a very broad question, and you might, consequently, be at a loss as to the approach you should take to answer it. If you've taken the time to think through and write a *Professional profile*, then a lot of the material within it can be recycled and repurposed to help you draft your answer to this question.

How do you write your *Professional profile*?

Your *Professional profile* should be about five to ten lines in length, and spark the reader's interest. If you can't successfully 'pitch' yourself in ten lines or less, you risk losing the reader's attention. Be persuasive. Be brief – you can highlight examples in later sections.

I would recommend that you don't use bullet points. Make a paragraph of it (just one paragraph). Your CV will be packed full of bullet points; it makes for a nice visual contrast to start with a paragraph.

I mentioned back in Chapter 3: Content and style: what to say and how to say it, that you should endeavour to write in the third person; however, if you really struggle to word your *Professional profile* in the third person, it is acceptable to use the first person.

If you decide to use bullet points then they should definitely be written in the third person. You should also try to keep it down to a maximum of five bullet points, and aim to use a different style of bullet point graphic than you have used within your *Career history*. Variety is the spice of life.

What to say?

I could talk about this subject for hours, but the very best way to illustrate how to write a *Professional profile* is to show you a couple of real-life examples.

EXAMPLE

An enthusiastic and self-motivated professional with extensive experience in financial services and investments. A skilled administrator who specialises in identifying and rectifying discrepancies and issues requiring accuracy and attention to detail at all times. Able to demonstrate an excellent working knowledge of the legislation appropriate to working in financial services with the proven ability to ensure full compliance therewith. Possesses excellent interpersonal skills and the ability to communicate concisely and articulately with clients and colleagues alike. Enjoys being part of a successful and productive team whilst demonstrating strong leadership potential in a highly competitive and demanding sector.

> ### EXAMPLE
>
> A dedicated and compassionate medical professional who specialises in the field of spinal neurosurgery. Able to demonstrate strong clinical expertise with the proven ability to assess and investigate patient symptoms and make appropriate decisions on the most appropriate treatment accordingly. Committed to the field of research and development with the aim of improving standards of medical practice through the use of technological advances. A valuable member, and leader, of a successful multidisciplinary team who thrives in highly pressurised and challenging working environments.

I'd also like to fire a small selection of adjectives, phrases and expressions at you. I must emphasise that these are only intended to help to get you thinking in the right direction. It's your *Professional profile*; you need to write it yourself. There is no set formula, but the following brief list should help your 'brainstorming' efforts:

- Dedicated
- Enthusiastic
- Positive
- Proactive
- Dynamic
- Versatile
- Professional
- Enjoys being part of, as well as leading, a successful and productive team.
- Proven track record in developing successful teams that exceed targets and objectives.
- Passionate about delivering an outstanding service whilst ensuring a commitment to achieving and exceeding targets and business objectives.
- Attentive to detail with a creative and innovative approach to problem solving and strategy development.
- Quick to grasp new ideas and concepts and to develop innovative and creative solutions to problems.

- Displays excellent problem-solving and interpersonal skills and can communicate concisely at all levels.
- Possesses excellent interpersonal skills and can communicate concisely at all levels from grassroots to board level.
- Utilises exceptional interpersonal skills and communicative abilities to build effective relationships with clients, suppliers and business colleagues.
- A confident communicator who is able to develop positive internal and external relationships.
- Can demonstrate the high levels of motivation required to meet the tightest of deadlines.
- Thrives in a fast-paced, results-driven environment.

A useful trick is to start off by writing a much longer version than you will actually need, including all the thoughts and ideas that spring to your mind. You can then edit it, rewrite it and cut it down until you eventually achieve the desired length. The text you're left with should be concise and powerful, focusing on the sales points that really matter.

Good writing is a lot like sculpture. You start with a great big block of marble and you steadily chip away at it bit by bit, until you've created your masterpiece.

Avoiding cliché and hyperbole

One of my clients once asked me, 'Aren't words such as "dedicated" and "enthusiastic" a waste of time? Would a recruiter call a client and say, "Hey, I've got a CV from somebody who is dedicated and enthusiastic."?'

She does have a point. No, recruiters wouldn't call up a client and proudly announce they've got a CV from someone who claims to be 'dedicated and enthusiastic'. They'd be intelligent enough to plug some of the candidate's more salient features. However, let's turn her question around and ask what a reader would think of a candidate who didn't say they were dedicated, enthusiastic etc. 'Enthusiastic' may be a rather overused word but it's also one of the very top characteristics employers look for.

It's clearly a fine line that you're going to have to tread, avoiding cliché and hyperbole. You are going to need to think very, very carefully how to phrase your *Professional profile*.

Case Study

Let's see how Jane chooses to tackle her *Professional profile*:

Professional profile

A positive, proactive and results-driven sales manager with a proven track record of profitable business growth through the creation of successful sales and marketing strategies. Experienced in working with leading brands in the competitive food and drink sector, focusing on exceeding customer service expectations, ensuring optimum brand impact. Possesses excellent interpersonal, communication and negotiation skills and the ability to develop and maintain mutually beneficial relationships with key decision makers.

BLOOPER!

To conclude this chapter, here's a few examples I have seen of precisely how NOT to phrase your *Professional profile*:

Well keen and up for everything that I'm interested in. Always on the go. Money, money, money! So enthusiastic for selling; it's in me to SELL, SELL, SELL! Able to persuade Eskimos to buy ice! I want a company car; I want to be out there in the field selling. Buying and selling is all I do and all I want to do. I'm going to achieve all my ambitions. From this day on I'm going to be rich. I know I sound up my own **** but sometimes you need to be to make and get yourself what you want for yourself and for the ones you love. I'm very funny, a great laugh. I've been told that I have a unique outlook on life. [We certainly wouldn't disagree with that last comment, would we?]

I am a 5'6" tall, stock Christian (yes, I actually do believe in God), dark hair with a goatee, fit and average weight.

I love arranging and planning and managing things. It all has to flow – like a river! I have an excellent track record – although I'm not a horse! [It's generally best to avoid trying to be humorous when writing a CV.]

A girl of bold, extrovert, charming personality with good administration skills – ready to serve the industry.

I will give a job my all as long as it doesn't interfere with my busy social life. My social life is very important to me.

I don't tend to procrastinate, except when the task is unpleasant or when I have to make a decision.

I always like to breathe in pleasant feelings around me ...

Chapter **7**

....

Objective

A *Professional profile* is often immediately followed by an *Objective* section. The task of the *Objective* section is to explain your preferred career direction and detail what you hope to achieve from your future career.

Should you include an *Objective* on your CV?

As with the *Professional profile*, I almost always advocate the inclusion of such a section, and as it is only a sentence or two in length there should normally be enough room to squeeze it in.

One could argue that there is plenty of room in the cover letter to cover the same ground. However, as with the *Professional profile*, don't forget that people reading your CV may not necessarily see your cover letter. Without the benefit of your cover letter it can be hard for them to deduce from your CV what it is that you're really looking for.

If you are aiming for a one-page CV and find that it's impossible to achieve without being detrimental to the presentation, then the *Objective* section can be axed to give you that little bit of extra room. It is better to have a one-page CV without an *Objective* than it is to have a one-page CV with an *Objective*.

One important case where an *Objective* is essential is if your current job isn't relevant to the one you are now looking for. To help to avoid any confusion on the part of the reader, you need to declare your future career intentions right at the beginning of your CV.

How do you write your *Objective*?

The style in which you write your *Objective* should match the style in which you've written your *Professional profile*. If you've used a paragraph format for your *Professional profile*, then you should use a paragraph format for your *Objective*. If, on the other hand, you've used bullet points for your *Professional profile* then your *Objective* should match this. Whilst variety is good, mixing and matching too many different styles can just look sloppy.

Your aim is to let the reader know what sort of position you are looking for and to give them another little taste of what you might be able to offer.

You should make reference to the specific job title of the role you wish to apply for without appearing contrived. For example, if you are applying in response to a vacancy for a 'Regional Head of Sales – Surrey' you would be ill-advised to say:

Now looking for a new and suitably challenging role as a Regional Head of Sales for Surrey

You would be much better off saying:

Now looking for a new and suitably challenging head of sales role

You've made mention of the key 'head of sales' words without appearing desperate for this one particular role!

Mentioning specific job titles is often advantageous, but be careful not to box yourself into a corner. Being too specific in your *Objective* could damage your chances if what you say you're looking for doesn't quite meet with what the reader thinks they're offering.

What to say?

As with your *Professional profile*, the very best way to illustrate how to write an *Objective* is to show you some real-life examples.

EXAMPLE

Currently looking for a new and challenging role as a QS, one which will make best use of existing skills and experience whilst enabling further personal and professional development.

Keen to achieve further professional development. Now looking to build on an extensive range of technical skills within a suitably challenging IT management role.

Currently in the market for a new and challenging position within the corporate sector, one which will make best use of experience acquired in privately owned companies whilst enabling further personal and professional development.

Now seeking a challenging new position, one which will make best use of existing legal knowledge and experience yet enable further personal and professional development. Keen to take up a new position, which will allow for further development within the legal arena.

You'll note that you don't just want to say what you're looking for; you want to seize this opportunity to pack in an additional sales pitch. Show the reader you're someone who is keen for a new challenge; keen to progress further. Show some enthusiasm!

Case Study

Here's how Jane handles her *Objective*:

Objective

Having successfully completed a BA (Hons) in Marketing and Advertising, now looking to return to the food and drink sector in a suitably challenging role. Keen to make best use of broad sales experience and strong theoretical knowledge of marketing and advertising.

BLOOPER!

And here are a couple of (real) examples of what you definitely should NOT say:

Although I trained as a solicitor and for the past ten years have developed a successful career in the legal sector, I am bored by it and hence wondered if you might have any other opportunities that may be of interest to me.

My goal was actually to be a psychologist but since I didn't go to university and get a qualification, I'll have to stick to working within PR.

Chapter **8**

Education and qualifications

Whilst not generally as important as the *Career history* section (it depends on the circumstances), the *Education and qualifications* section is, nevertheless, a very important section in most CVs.

If you've just graduated and have little work experience, then the *Education and qualifications* section is going to be of greater interest than your *Career history*. However, if you've already been out in the workplace for some time then it's normally your *Career history* that is going to be more important to a recruiter.

Focusing on what matters

When writing a CV you should always focus on more recent history and summarise older information. Recruiters will be most interested in what has happened most recently and, conversely, less interested in what came before, although they obviously still need to know the basics of older information.

For example, if you've got A levels, then don't list all your GCSEs or O levels on the CV.

And if your qualifications are limited to a handful of O levels passed in the 1960s, then why mention them at all? They have absolutely no relevance to your current employability and you're under no obligation to include them.

In the same spirit of focusing on what matters, you should always work in reverse chronological order, i.e. start with your most recent qualification and work backwards. To read more about the concept of reverse chronological order please refer back to Chapter 4: Structure: which type of CV is right for you?

Structure

You want to structure this section clearly, so you could use bullet points or a table, or maybe a mixture of the two, to lay out the information.

You need to specify:

➤ The dates you received your qualifications, or attended the relevant institutions.

➤ Descriptions of your qualifications, e.g. BSc (Hons) Veterinary Medicine.

➤ What grades/class/marks you achieved if applicable.

➤ If deemed sufficiently relevant, the names of the institution(s).

Dates

Dates are normally required. However, if the most recent qualifications go back a long way then it's fine to omit the dates.

Descriptions of qualifications

Make sure that you state the precise, formal title of the qualifications you have gained. For example, Maths should always be spelled out in full, e.g. Mathematics.

Grades/class/marks

There's not normally any requirement to list grades in full unless they're a major selling point. For example, if you've got a degree then there's no need to include A-level grades unless they're all As or Bs. The reader is going to be far more interested in the degree than the A levels.

You could see this as simply being concise or you could see this as being economical with the truth. It all depends on your point of view and your own precise circumstances.

TOP TIP

A situation where you can definitely be economical with the truth is when you have a degree but only achieved a 2:2 or a 3rd. It's not going to add anything to your saleability to quote the degree class; the fact that you graduated is a strong enough selling point on its own. Of course, if you got a 1st or a 2:1 then that's a different matter because that would clearly be a strong selling point.

An exception to these rules would be the legal professions. The sheer competitiveness of the sector means that recruiters may want to look at your academic background in great detail. As such, a legal CV should be very comprehensive in this respect, including full details of institutions attended, grades achieved etc. at all levels of study.

Institution names

If you have any qualifications gained at university then you should always name the universities concerned. However, with the exception of legal CVs, unless you previously attended a particularly well-known school or college, it is generally not necessary to provide its name. As with everything else on your CV, if they're not selling points, leave them out.

If you're not a graduate then by all means list the name of the school or college you most recently attended, but it's not necessary to list the names of all the institutions you attended. Your prospective employer really won't care.

Case study

Jane summarises her qualifications as follows:

Education and qualifications	
BA (Hons):	Marketing and Advertising, University of Sussex (2009)
3 A Levels:	English, English Literature and French (1997)
10 GCSEs:	Including English and Mathematics (1995)

Further training

I'd often recommend following the main *Education and qualifications* section with either a *Further training* and/or a *Further skills* section. Inclusion of this will depend on whether or not you have undertaken additional training subsequent to your formal qualifications and whether or not you can demonstrate specific additional skills for which you have no formal qualification.

The *Further training* or *Vocational training* (or maybe even *Technical training* or *Continuing professional development*) section should make mention of useful classes and courses you have undertaken during the course of your career. Employers place a lot of value on continuing professional development (CPD); in many professions (medical, teaching etc.) you are expected to be continually learning. I'm not saying you should necessarily list every class, course or seminar. If you've attended them by the dozen then focus on those which will be of the greatest interest to a prospective employer.

EXAMPLE

Further training

- Management Development Programme
- Marketing Management
- Presentation Skills
- Finance for Non-Financial Managers
- Effective Man Management
- Appraisal Training
- Team Building
- Creativity Training

Qualifications such as NVQs are best listed within your main *Education and qualifications* section, whereas professional qualifications such as the European Computer Driving Licence (ECDL) and the RSA Computer Literacy and Information Technology (CLAIT) qualifications are best placed within *Further training*.

Case study

Jane has undertaken a couple of valuable courses and lists them as follows:

Further training

- CLAIT Level 1: Including optional unit in Database Manipulation (2009)
- Commercial Awareness & Marketing Intelligence (2007)

Further skills

The *Further skills* section can be used to provide details of IT skills, linguistic skills etc.

On the subject of IT skills, ensure you get the names, spacing and capitalisation of IT packages correct, e.g. QuarkXPress, PowerPoint (this convention is known as 'CamelCase' or medial capitals, BiCapitalisation, CapWords and InterCaps, and originated within the IT sector, although it has now spread to other areas). If in doubt, check!

Case study

Following completion of her CLAIT course, Jane has a range of valuable IT skills, and, having lived in France for a time, speaks French fluently. She also studied German at GCSE and can still 'get by'.

Further skills

IT Skills: MS Office including PowerPoint & Access, QuarkXPress and PhotoShop
Languages: Fluent French; basic German

Language skills are always of interest to employers and your level should be specified as basic, intermediate/conversational or fluent.

If the only skills you need to highlight within the *Further skills* section are IT skills then you can simply retitle the section *IT skills* or *Key IT skills* and bullet point the list.

EXAMPLE

IT skills

- MS Office including PowerPoint & Access, QuarkXPress and PhotoShop

---

However, if your IT skills are extensive (for example, you work within IT) then it's best to make them easier to scan by breaking them down by category; for example, hardware, software, programming languages, network protocols.

You should also highlight your accreditation with Microsoft, Cisco etc.

Other information you could place under *Further skills* include details of driving licences if that is of particular importance to your work; for example, if you're a HGV driver. However, generally this is best left to the *Other details* section that we'll come to in a later chapter.

If you are in a nonmedical profession and have completed an appropriate First Aid at Work qualification, then you could also include this under *Further skills*. Or you could just include it under *Other details* (see Chapter 12: Other details). It's up to you!

Chapter **9**

Career history

The *Career history* section is, in most cases, the most important section of a CV. The exception being those individuals with little or no work experience, for example, recent school leavers and graduates.

There are a variety of possible headings for this section that you can use instead of *Career history*. If you feel the word 'career' isn't applicable to your circumstances, or if you are a recent graduate and haven't even started your career, then you might prefer to say *Employment history* or *Work experience*.

Whatever you choose to call the section, the basic principles stay the same.

Focusing on what matters

Just like your *Education and qualifications*, you should always work in reverse chronological order (start with your present or most recent job and work all the way back to your very first job).

As with the *Education and qualifications* section, focus on recent information and summarise older information. Your current or most recent job should always have the most detail.

Prospective employers are interested in points that are most relevant to them, so be concise when describing roles that aren't particularly relevant to the job you are applying for, and, conversely, make sure that you highlight and elaborate on any roles that are relevant.

> **TOP TIP**
>
> If you have a multi-page CV, ensure that your current or most recent employment features on the first page.

If you're struggling to fit your CV onto the recommended maximum of two pages, then it is very likely that you are putting too much detail into your *Career history*.

Structure

You need to specify:

➤ The name of the organisation you worked for, along with its location.

➤ The dates you worked for each organisation.

➤ Your job title or function, e.g. head of marketing.

➤ A compelling description of what your role entailed.

Dates

Unexplained gaps in your employment record can raise concerns in the minds of recruiters. They may think you have something to hide!

A useful trick is to cover up brief chronological gaps by listing only years, not months, within your *Career history*. I'd recommend doing this regardless of whether or not you have any gaps. I consider listing all the months to be unnecessary detail. Some recruiters, especially some recruitment agencies, still insist on all the months being listed. Medical professionals should always provide full details.

If you have larger gaps that can't be concealed by simply omitting the months then that can be problematic. But there are solutions, which we'll cover in Chapter 15: Ten solutions for ten potential problems.

And if you're still in the role then you can use the term 'to date'. For example, '2007– to date'.

Your job title or function

This is fairly self-explanatory. My only word of warning is not to embellish. Remember: the prospective employer may well contact previous employers for references and you don't want the prospective employer to refer to you as a project manager when you were in fact just an assistant project manager!

Details of the organisation you worked for

There are only a few types of organisation you are likely to have worked for.

The two most common are a private limited company and a public limited company.

Most small and medium enterprises (SMEs) in the UK are private limited companies, and SMEs employ a very large proportion of the country's workforce.

A public limited company is normally a much larger enterprise; Sainsbury's the supermarket ('J Sainsbury plc'), for example. Whilst there may be fewer public limited companies than private limited companies, they employ a significant proportion of the population because their workforces are generally very large, often tens of thousands.

The 'Limited' part of the name of a private limited company can be abbreviated to 'Ltd' to save space, but the initial letter 'L' should always be capitalised. Do not put a full stop.

On the other hand, 'plc' (public limited company) should be written in lower case, and, as with Ltd, should never have a full stop after it.

Ltd can be written as ltd, and plc can also be written PLC (but not Plc), but Ltd and plc are the most common usages.

As regards location, it is sufficient to list the town or city (if abroad, the country). There's no need for a full address.

A compelling description of what your role entailed

Not a dry and boring job description!

You'd be surprised how many people copy and paste their official job description into their CV. This is most definitely not recommended, especially when the original has spelling or grammatical errors!

This is the most important content in your *Career history* and you have to get it right.

When describing your main duties and responsibilities, try to give specific examples where possible. Including brief but relevant examples of how you meet the prospective employer's criteria can make a big difference to the credibility of your words.

This is the place to really emphasise what it was that you achieved in each role (bearing in mind that you might also decide to have a separate *Achievements* section – see Chapter 11: Achievements).

Pay attention to the order in which you list your bullet points. They should be listed in a logical order, grouping together similar items, and your greatest selling points should come first. This is another reason for not simply copying your official job description; they frequently focus on what you spend most of your time doing, not what is most important.

TOP TIP

Don't feel you should only include paid, permanent employment. Relevant unpaid or temporary work can be a valuable addition to your CV. It all depends on precisely what it was you did – and how you choose to describe it.

Unnecessary detail

I often see salary details and/or 'reason for leaving' detailed under each job on people's CVs. Don't do this. It's superfluous, unnecessary detail.

Salary is always a sensitive issue. You shouldn't bring it up in your CV or at an interview, wait until a firm job offer is being negotiated. Providing precise details of your salary in advance is inappropriate and can potentially serve to weaken your position when it comes to negotiating the salary package you are now looking for. Unless you have specifically been asked to include such information on your CV, leave it out. If an employer really wants to know details of your salary history they can always ask when they interview you.

Your reasons for leaving a job can also be a delicate matter to handle, and are often hard to explain concisely. Why take up valuable room on your CV explaining your reasons for leaving when that space could be better spent incorporating additional sales points? Most recruiters won't be expecting your reasons for leaving to be detailed on your CV, and if they really want to know, then the interview is the appropriate time for such issues to be discussed.

BLOOPER!

• •

One lady really laid into her current employer on her CV, stating what a complete ***** she was and how badly she was verbally abused on an almost daily basis. This was undoubtedly a very unfortunate situation for her, but making an issue of it in her CV was definitely not doing her any favours getting a new job!

Career summary and *Key experience*

Instead of a full *Career history*, you may wish to consider using a *Career summary*. This is perhaps most appropriate if you have opted for a functional or hybrid CV. (For a detailed explanation of the different types of CV, see Chapter 4: Structure: which type of CV is right for you?)

If you have a long and varied *Career history* and are now looking to change career path then the best approach might be to start by writing a normal *Career history* and then divide it up into three separate sections:

➤ *Key experience*

➤ *Current employment*

➤ *Career summary*

This will help to dilute the attention which might be focused on any particular role.

Within the *Key experience* section you should highlight aspects of your career history that are most relevant to the role you are now looking to undertake, possibly split into separate subheadings.

The *Current employment* section can give comprehensive details of your current role, which is always of interest to a prospective employer.

The *Career summary* needs to list only dates, job titles and employers' names and locations; there is no need to include details of duties, responsibilities and achievements.

EXAMPLE

Key experience

Team management

- Managing the recruitment and selection process to ensure that appropriately qualified and experienced staff are hired in accordance with business requirements
- Conducting regular staff appraisals and providing constructive feedback to facilitate progression and performance improvements in line with business development plans
- Encouraging all members of staff to support company strategies and initiatives whilst ensuring that they remain focused on providing a world class standard of service
- Coordinating the provision of comprehensive training to all staff to ensure that they have the knowledge and capabilities required to fulfil their job roles to the very best of their abilities
- Adopting a supportive management style that encourages staff at all levels to openly discuss any concerns they may have and working collaboratively to facilitate their resolution

Performance management

- Chairing and documenting weekly management team meetings to monitor the achievement of KPIs
- Developing and executing innovative strategies designed to achieve increased market share in a competitive industry as well as implementing local and central marketing activities
- Taking appropriate action to resolve any issues identified following a review of internal management systems
- Playing a pivotal role in ensuring that all employees comply fully with company procedures and industry specific legislation
- Completing audits and risk assessments with the aim of ensuring full compliance with health, safety and security guidelines and legislation

Business management

- Providing a visible management presence for customers and maximising all opportunities to interact with them thereby encouraging repeat business
- Proactively seeking feedback from customers as well as reviewing customer attendance information and taking appropriate steps to drive improvements
- Conducting thorough investigations into any complaints that may arise and providing solutions that are satisfactory to the business and the customer
- Travelling extensively to review performance and standards in company and competitor units and identifying areas for improvement in terms of revenue growth within the unit

Recent career history and *Previous employment*

If you are worried that your age may be counting against you, the best technique is to place the focus very firmly on your most recent history and to radically summarise earlier information.

To achieve this, you can split your *Career history* into a *Recent career history* section spanning the past decade or so and a *Previous employment* section. The former can go into appropriate detail, and the latter should list job titles, employers' names and locations without dates or details of duties, responsibilities and achievements.

Employment history and *Work experience*

Even if you have little or no work experience – you may only have worked to help to fund your studies – it is still worth mentioning. Some workplace experience is always better than none.

Case study

Let's look at how Jane describes her current role:

Career summary

2007–date   Sales Manager, ABC Stationery plc, London
- Playing a key role within a large stationery retailer, tasked with the redevelopment of the sales strategy across the UK market
- Planning and executing innovative campaigns, including direct mail and telesales
- Personally cold calling to bring on board high profile – and credit-worthy – new clients
- Liaising extensively with clients to agree product specifications, sale prices and lead times
- Building mutually beneficial relationships with suppliers, negotiating terms and discounts
- Interviewing, recruiting, training and mentoring new sales executives into the business
- Setting budgets and forecasting sales whilst maintaining full P&L accountability

She will also be adding some achievements to this but we'll come on to that in Chapter 11: Achievements.

Chapter **10**

Key skills

So, what is a *Key skills* section exactly? It's often misunderstood.

A *Key skills* section is a summary of the main skills and abilities you are offering a prospective employer, your top selling points in terms of skills and abilities.

It shouldn't be confused with an *Achievements* section (which we'll cover in the next chapter). An *Achievements* section will focus on your experience rather than your pure skills and abilities.

Should you include a *Key skills* section on your CV?

One school of thought suggests that by including a *Key skills* section on the first page it's impossible for recruiters to miss it, or at least very hard for them to ignore it. However, the inclusion of a *Key skills* section in a CV is becoming less popular these days. It is now generally considered better to spread evidence of key skills and abilities throughout your *Career history*. This is a more powerful and convincing approach. (You can also address specific points in the cover letter, a vitally important part of any application.)

However, a *Key skills* section remains essential for the functional CV type.

What to include

Recent school leavers and graduates can pick out skills they've acquired during their studies and feature them as bullet points within a *Key skills* section, regardless of whether or not they've had a chance to apply them in the workplace.

And if you're adopting the functional CV approach because your previous experience is not directly relevant to the role you are now seeking, then you should make use of the *Key skills* section to focus on the transferable skills and abilities that you have developed during the course of your career.

If you can, try to break up your key skills under separate subheadings, grouping together related items in a logical fashion.

For example, you could have different headings for:

➤ Communication skills
➤ Interpersonal skills

- Administrative skills
- Organisational skills
- Negotiation skills
- Presentation skills
- Research skills
- Numerical skills

This is just a selection of ideas for possible headings rather than a precise formula. You will need to list all your own skills, bearing in mind the demands of the job for which you are applying, and then seek to categorise them as best suits your own personal circumstances.

Talking of the importance of taking into consideration the requirements of the job for which you are applying, the *Key skills* section is always an area to consider tailoring carefully for each individual application. Whilst you should be subtle about this and not simply repeat everything which has been listed in the person specification, you should ensure that you cover all the bases.

Key strengths

An alternative approach which I occasionally see is a *Key strengths* section. This is often used as a way to combine the *Key skills* and *Achievements* sections but it may also be used in addition. Essentially, it takes particular skills and abilities and backs them up with evidence and examples. (Many people mistakenly mix up the terms *Key strengths* and *Key skills* but the difference is clear – a *Key strengths* section contains a lot more background information.)

My professional opinion is that:

- A *Key skills* section is generally not necessary (except for functional and mixed CVs).
- An *Achievements* section is highly recommended (see next chapter).
- Any ideas you have for *Key strengths* would be best placed in your *Career summary*.

However, as always, there are exceptions to the rules, and depending on your career history and your precise mix of key skills and achievements, you may feel you would be best served by a *Key strengths* section.

It shouldn't take long to knock up drafts of both versions and you can then get a clear idea as to which approach works best for you.

BLOOPER!

· ·

I know I've included a lot of real-life examples in this book which defy belief, but I promise I haven't invented any of them! I have seen thousands upon thousands of CVs, so there are inevitably going to be some really cracking blunders in amongst them. The following example *Key skills* section is certainly no exception.

Strengths:

➤ Pretty

➤ Lovely Smile

➤ Nice Puppies

➤ Cute Bum

Weaknesses:

➤ A couple of brown tramlines inside thighs

➤ Inability to frown

I was very tempted to tell the owner of this particular CV that she should perhaps consider writing this in prose instead of bullet points: 'I am a pretty little thing with nice puppies and a cute bum, although I have been told that I have curious brown tramlines inside my thighs.' However, I erred on the side of caution and politely suggested that she might be better off leaving out the section entirely.

For the avoidance of any possible doubt, you should definitely not subdivide your *Key skills* section into 'Strengths' and 'Weaknesses'. Weaknesses have no place in your CV; it's the strengths we're interested in!

Chapter **11**

Achievements

Including an *Achievements* (or *Accomplishments*) section in a CV is by no means compulsory and there are many instances where it simply won't apply. But if you can include such a section then it could really make an instant and dramatic difference to the power of your CV. It helps prevent your *Career history* from reading too much like a job description and it gives you an opportunity to distinguish yourself from other candidates.

This is no time for false modesty. This is a time to show what you have achieved and to imply that you will be capable of achieving similar results in the future.

The one goal of your CV is to get you an interview and this one addition to your CV will undoubtedly help to get you noticed, leading to more interview invitations.

'Achievements' is a powerful and positive word and it will immediately convey a powerful and positive impression of you to the reader. It differentiates you from other, average candidates. Given the competition you are likely to be facing, being average will not get you the job. You have to set yourself apart. Too many above-average candidates let themselves down with a below-average CV.

Integrating achievements into your CV

You might choose to have either one collective *Achievements* section in your CV, or if you feel you have enough to warrant it, you can even have separate *Achievements* subheadings under each role in your *Career history*. Whichever you choose, it is worth noting that you should be careful to avoid repetition in your CV. If you have something to say then say it once – and once only. Space is always at a premium.

> **TOP TIP**
>
> A word of warning for more mature candidates: if you have an extensive *Career history* then make sure you limit your entries to recent achievements. Don't go back any further than the past decade or so.

What words to use

You must be economical with your words. If you want your statements to have the maximum impact then they need to be concise. Don't pad out your bullet points with superfluous detail and explanations; you'll lose momentum.

You may recall that 'achieved' is one of the action verbs we talked about in Chapter 3: Content and style: what to say and how to say it. Please refer back to this chapter for further ideas on how best to express yourself. You may also like to take a look at Appendix A: 250 action verbs, for further ideas.

What are employers looking for?

To help trigger your thought processes, here are some examples of contributions employers expect their employees to make:

➤ Increase: profits; sales/turnover, working capital, market share, efficiency

➤ Decrease: costs, waste, excess stock, timescales, complaints, staff turnover

➤ Improve: cashflow, procedures, performance, teamwork, reputation, PR

➤ Arrange: change, innovation, events, results

Think back through your career and identify instances where you have made such contributions.

I have summarised these ideas under four headings: increase, decrease, improve and arrange. However, you will be able to add diversity to your statements by making use of the broad range of action verbs in Appendix A: 250 action verbs.

Quantify

In Chapter 3: Content and style: what to say and how to say it, I also discussed the importance of backing up your claims.

Here are some examples for you:

If you weren't solely and personally responsible for a particular achievement but supported a team or another individual in doing so, then don't hold back; you're entitled to credit for it too!

EXAMPLE

Delivered a substantial increase in weekly sales levels, from £45,000 to £85,000 – nearly doubling sales

Personally responsible for delivering the highest sales contribution for the group of 24.4%, with the closest rival delivering just 15.8%

Won the Deputy Manager of the Year Award in 2008, resulting in promotion to the management of the flagship Liverpool branch

Successfully drove down stock from £1.5 million to £800k in just nine months whilst maintaining lead times, consequently boosting working capital by £700k

Increased market share from 12% to 15% over an 18-month period – an increase of 25%

Personally achieved a 34% increase in uptake of after-sales insurance packages

Improved production line procedures, reducing producing time by 12%, raising efficiency and reducing costs

Successfully reducing VAT reconciliation discrepancies from £6 million to just £25k

Played a key role within the team responsible for smashing the previous regional sales record by an impressive 37%

Case study

Jane thinks back through her career and identifies the following achievements she can include in her CV:

- Led the introduction of a major culture change in customer service, improving customer satisfaction ratings from 6.2 out of 10 to 8.3 out of 10

- Boosted regional sales levels by nearly 35% over a 2 year period with no additional marketing spend

- Organised a successful new product launch, gaining a substantial amount of local and national press coverage

- Featured in the programme *Business Lunch* on XYZ TV, providing invaluable exposure for the business

Personal achievements can also be important

As well as highlighting achievements from your professional and academic life, you should also consider including personal achievements, as these help to reflect your personality and add that little extra something, which will help to differentiate you from your competition. We'll cover personal achievements in greater detail in Chapter 13: Interests and activities.

Chapter **12**

Other details

The *Other details* section is somewhat of a mixed bag. Use it to make mention of any bits and pieces that don't readily fit into other sections or aren't sufficiently important to merit inclusion within other sections.

Driving licence

Details of your driving licence should always be included on your CV, even if your licence isn't 'clean'. Under normal circumstances you can describe it as being 'Full/Clean' or 'Provisional/Clean'. However, if you have any points on your licence, then simply describe it as 'Full' (or 'Provisional' if applicable). It's obviously going to be rather negative to list the number of points you have (as some people do). And if you've been banned then you should avoid making any mention of your licence (or lack of) whatsoever.

Please note, if driving is vital to your work, for example, if you're a HGV driver, then you can 'promote' mention of your licence(s) to a *Further skills* section.

TOP TIP

Remember that the correct spelling is 'licence' and not 'license'.

Health

Should you include details of your health? Whether or not you smoke?

Well, you certainly shouldn't state that you are a smoker or have any health problems on the CV itself; however, if your health is excellent and you're a non-smoker, mention it if there is space. Don't try to force it in if you can think of something more constructive to include.

If you have a recognised disability then the Equality Act 2010 normally prevents a prospective employer from discriminating against you on these grounds. Unfortunately, however, the reality is that some employers will flout the law; therefore, I recommend you wait until you attend interview to disclose any disability. If your disability is not immediately obvious to an employer when you attend the interview, you can wait until you receive a firm job offer.

You should note that because there are certain exceptions to the rules regarding discriminating on the basis of disability, it is entirely permissible for employers to question you on this subject at interview.

First aid

If you have completed an appropriate first aid qualification then *Other details* is the place to make mention of it. It's all grist to your mill. Alternatively, if you've implemented a *Further skills* section (see Chapter 8: Education and qualifications) you may decide this is the more appropriate place.

Professional registration

The *Other details* section is the place to provide details of any professional registration, including reference numbers. But don't include details of your hepatitis B status; it's jumping the gun.

Professional memberships

You should highlight any relevant professional affiliations, such as membership of the British Computer Society. They're valuable selling points.

Many sectors now offer the opportunity to become a member of a professional organisation with various different levels of membership achievable, and becoming a member of a professional organisation provides external recognition of your competence.

Nationality

As we've already established in a previous chapter, it's not recommended to include your nationality because of the risk of discrimination. However, if you are a citizen of a country outside the European Union (EU), then you can highlight your right to work in the UK. It will assuage any concerns a prospective employer may have on this front.

Relocation

If you're applying for a vacancy that is clearly beyond reasonable commuting distance of your current residence, then it can be helpful to indicate on your CV that you are prepared to relocate. In some cases this will be essential; for example, a British company might be advertising for someone to oversee their expansion into China, with the successful applicant being based in the Shanghai office.

EXAMPLE

Relocation: Prepared to relocate for the right opportunity

Holiday plans

One candidate that came to us for help, having achieved very little success with her own CV, had specified within the *Other details* section of her CV her holiday plans for the next three years, and made it quite clear that she would not be changing them and that any prospective employer would have to accommodate them! Her annual trips were very important to her.

First of all, imposing these kinds of restrictions on a prospective employer isn't going to be to your advantage. And second, the *Other details* section of your CV is definitely not the place to communicate this sort of information. It should be saved for the cover letter, or, preferably, the interview. By that stage you've got your foot in the door and an employer who is keen to have you on board is more likely to make a greater effort to accommodate such stipulations. But don't count on it!

We completely removed all mention of holidays from this candidate's CV (and made quite a number of other changes), advised her to raise the issue at interview instead. She managed to secure a new job within a couple of weeks, and her new employer was prepared to accept her holiday commitments for the year ahead, albeit not the full three years she had insisted upon. Sometimes you have to know when to compromise!

Interests and activities

We'll be discussing the *Interests and activities* section of your CV in the next chapter. However, I would just like to mention here that if you aren't planning to include such a section because you don't feel there's enough room then there is an alternative approach. You can simply summarise your interests in one line under *Other details*. For example, 'Interests include: x, y and z'.

EXAMPLE

Interests include: badminton, squash, Pilates, theatre & amateur dramatics and cinema

---

Referees

Details of referees shouldn't be included on your CV. They're a waste of valuable space! They clutter it up, and, more importantly, you will find that your referees get pestered unnecessarily by time wasters. By the time they have handled their umpteenth enquiry of the day, they are a lot less likely to say nice things about you!

A simple statement at the bottom of your CV saying, 'References are available on request,' is more than sufficient, because it's not information that a recruiter needs to have up front. When your application progresses to the next level and there is serious talk of a job offer, then that is the time to provide those details.

The main exception to this rule is when you are specifically instructed to provide details of referees with your initial application. Some employers will insist on having details of referees up front, as will some recruitment agencies.

If you have been specifically instructed to do so then you have little choice but to comply. However, it's not normally necessary to have to squeeze this extra information into your CV. If you've spent time perfecting the layout of your CV, then adding in all this extra information is likely to be quite time consuming, not to mention detrimental to the impact of your CV. You should provide full details on a separate sheet matching in style with your CV.

There are other exceptions, such as medical CVs, for example, and we'll cover these in Chapter 16: Special cases – professions where the rules are different.

Handling convictions

Undoubtedly, a criminal conviction is going to be difficult to handle.

> **BLOOPER!**
> ●
>
> Explaining a conviction by simply saying, 'I killed my wife,' is not going to get you invited to an interview! (You won't believe me, but one candidate did put this on his CV.)

The solution is simple. Don't make any mention of criminal convictions. You are not under any obligation to disclose convictions unless:

➤ you are specifically asked to do so, or

➤ you are applying for one of a small number of special cases.

The Rehabilitation of Offenders Act 1974 allows for certain criminal convictions to be deemed 'spent' after what is termed a 'rehabilitation period'. If a criminal conviction is spent then you are permitted to conceal it from a prospective employer, and if you have any criminal convictions then it is vital to be aware of what the applicable rehabilitation period is.

The Act also makes it unlawful for record-keeping bodies such as the Criminal Records Bureau to disclose details of such convictions.

However, these rules do not apply to certain employers and organisations. The rationale is to ensure that employers and organisations offering certain sensitive positions, professions and licences can access an applicant's full criminal history before reaching a decision.

If you are in any doubt as regards your own specific circumstances then it's always best to seek appropriate professional advice.

Case study

Jane's circumstances are very simple. She has a full clean driving licence and she's a non-smoker in excellent health.

Other details	
Driving Licence:	Full/Clean
Health:	Excellent; non-smoker

Chapter **13**

Interests and activities

There's always a lot of debate about the *Interests and activities* section. In this chapter I'll outline the pros and cons of including such a section, explain my opinion on the matter and detail precisely how you should handle your *Interests and activities* section – if you decide to include one.

Should you or shouldn't you?

Before we discuss what to, or, perhaps more importantly, what not to include in this section, let's ask ourselves whether or not you should even bother including such a section on your CV.

As with many other aspects of your CV, there are reasons for and reasons against.

First let's look at the reasons *against* including such a section.

➤ Space is normally at a premium, so it is vital to prioritise and only include information which will help to make your case. Are your hobbies and pastimes relevant?

➤ A number of surveys have resulted in comments from recruiters that *Interests and activities* sections are 'a waste of space' and 'tiresome and tedious'.

➤ A trained recruiter should disregard this section when shortlisting because it's technically of no relevance to the candidature and is notorious for including exaggerations and mistruths.

STATISTIC

An interesting survey by the Recruitment & Employment Confederation found that 71 per cent of recruiters had actually decided not to shortlist a candidate purely as a result of information they put under *Interests and activities*.

Now let's tackle the reasons why you *should* include such a section.

➤ Whilst nobody has yet conducted a survey specifically to research this, there is plenty of anecdotal evidence of recruiters deciding to call someone in for an interview purely as a result of what they've included on their CV under *Interests and activities*. I, for one, will admit to having done so when hiring.

➤ We are naturally attracted to people who share our own interests in life, so if your interests match those of the recruiters reading your CV, there is a high probability it will increase your chances of their interviewing you.

➤ Without an *Interests and activities* section, a CV can be rather a cold, lifeless document. Including brief details of what you do outside office hours can bring a much-needed personal touch.

➤ Sifting through large piles of CVs can be very tedious indeed, and reading the *Interests and activities* sections can make the task that little bit more interesting for the recruiter.

➤ Anything (within reason) that can help your CV stand out from the crowd and grab the reader's attention could give you an advantage over other potential candidates.

➤ Whilst saying that you enjoy 'socialising' might come across as a 'tiresome and tedious waste of space' in the eyes of a recruiter, with a little thought and effort you should be able to come up with some more imaginative alternatives.

➤ Giving an interviewer the opportunity to talk about your *Interests and activities* can be an excellent ice-breaker.

➤ Besides knowing whether you're capable of actually doing the job, most employers are keen to know what sort of a person you would be like to work alongside. Yes, they can get an idea at interview but your *Interests and activities* can also give them some insight.

➤ Employers are generally keen to have a diversity of characters within their team and are always on the lookout for someone who can add a new dimension to the team.

So what to conclude?

Yes, I have listed more reasons for including an *Interests and activities* section than I have listed not to include one. And, for the time being, I remain firmly convinced that you most certainly should include such a section on your CV. But – and this is very important – you most certainly should not go overboard. Keep it short. Keep it simple. Don't write a whole essay about what you do in your spare time.

Graduates, in particular, often fall foul on this point, not infrequently devoting up to half an A4 page to their 'extracurricular' activities. Writing far too much under *Interests and activities* is a common mistake I see.

Detailed explanations are best saved for the interview stage. For one thing, you want to avoid giving the impression that your hobbies are more important to you than your career. If a prospective employer fears that your hobbies may well end up taking priority over your work life, then that is definitely not going to count in your favour.

Information that is directly relevant to the position you are applying for should always take precedence, but, space allowing, an *Interests and activities* section rounds off a CV nicely and helps to bring it to life just at the point the reader is about to make that critical decision whether or not to invite the applicant for interview.

STATISTIC

Statistics reveal a trend over the past ten years of an increasing number of people choosing to omit such a section, so a time may come when this section of a CV becomes history. But until the majority of job hunters decide not to include their *Interests and activities*, this is one instance where I would recommend 'going with the herd'.

It's far from compulsory, though. If you really feel that you have nothing to say in this section (perhaps your work is your life), then you have little choice but to leave it out.

Leaving it out can also be a useful little trick to gain a little bit of extra space on your CV if you're finding it difficult to fit everything else in without it appearing cramped.

As mentioned in the previous chapter, you can simply summarise your interests in one line under *Other details*. For example, 'Interests include: x, y and z', instead of dedicating an entire separate section to them.

Extracurricular activities are of particular interest to recruiters who work with the teaching professions. Recruiters will be looking for evidence that you really want to get involved with all aspects of school life, contribute to the community and build relationships with the students both in and out of the classroom. In this case, an *Interests and activities* section is vital.

What to put, or, perhaps more importantly, what not to put

Not everyone will have enough spare time to indulge in any hobbies. Between the demands of modern working and family life, many people's idea of a hobby is having five minutes spare to watch *Coronation Street*!

Popular as they may be, you should definitely look to exclude certain activities that are guaranteed not to impress a prospective employer.

➤ Socialising (consistently voted No.1 most common entry in this section)

➤ Watching TV/going shopping (undoubtedly the most uninteresting!)

➤ Listening to music (very common and hardly sounds very interesting)

➤ Clubbing

➤ Travel

BLOOPER!

One graduate put on his CV: 'I like to watch *EastEnders* and *Ugly Betty*.'

As always, there are exceptions. If you're looking to work in the travel sector then you should definitely make mention of your interest in travelling, and if you're planning to work in a night club then it's acceptable to state your passion for clubbing. But in the vast majority of cases you should leave these out.

Relevancy

In an ideal world some of your interests would be relevant in some way to your job. If you are engaged in an activity which could be considered to have a connection with your work then you should certainly make a feature of this. Membership of relevant amateur societies and clubs is always a bonus, and any team activities are likely to be relevant to almost any job.

Be specific

It is a good idea to try to 'qualify' your interests. For example, just saying 'Cooking' isn't going to be particularly interesting to the reader, but 'Cooking (French and Italian)' is immediately much more memorable.

Positions of responsibility

It's always a good idea if you can subtly slip in mention of any positions of responsibility you hold outside work. If your passion is, for example, football, and you're also the captain of the local team, then do say so on your CV:

> *Football (captain of local team)*

Besides the obvious selling point of football being a team activity (and hence your being a 'team player'), you've immediately communicated your leadership qualities, your ability to take responsibility for others, your ability to commit yourself to a project etc.

Personal achievements

As well as flagging up your professional achievements on your CV, don't be modest when it comes to your personal achievements. Personal achievements demonstrate talent and commitment just as much, if not more so than professional achievements. Imagine you've won the Celeste Art Prize for your oil paintings, or perhaps you've excelled at some particular sport. Remember, as with everything else on your CV, try to keep the focus on recent history. There's no point in going too far back; the older the information, the weaker its impact.

Voluntary work

If you're actively involved in any voluntary work then *Interests and activities* is the ideal place to make mention of this. This sort of activity should count in your favour with many employers. Not only does it show that you are civil-minded, but it also indicates that you most likely have strong people skills. Don't be afraid to blow your own trumpet; just keep it short and to the point.

Unusual hobbies

Mainstream interests, such as horse riding, for example, have the advantage that you're more likely to stumble upon a recruiter who shares the same interest. Conversely, it is probably unlikely that anyone reading your CV will share your interest in lizard breeding; however, that's not to say you wouldn't be invited for an interview anyway just to get a closer look at you! So there may be some advantage to displaying some originality in this section. It's a lottery really, and there's no firm advice I can give other than to avoid mentioning any interests which may cause offence among certain readers, for example, hunting.

Don't go over the top

Whatever you do include, you should be able to back it up. If you mention chess to give your CV some intellectual clout but haven't actually played since you were at school, then you could well come a cropper in your interview if your interviewer turns out to be a chess fan and asks you which openings to the game you favour!

BLOOPER!

Putting 'Golf' on your CV to impress a corporate recruiter when you have in fact only been on a golf course twice in your entire life could be something that you come to regret in the future when your new manager is looking to organise a golfing weekend.

Order

You should give some thought to the order in which you list your *Interests and activities*. Try to group them logically. For instance, instead of 'Football, film/cinema, tennis and creative writing', try 'Football, tennis, film/cinema and creative writing', i.e. keep sports together, outdoor activities together and indoor or more cerebral activities together. It will read better that way.

Humour

Finally, I would firmly caution against humour. You might think it shows a sense of humour to say you enjoy 'going out with mates every single night'. But the reader probably won't find this particularly funny.

BLOOPER!

I once saw a CV where the gentleman had simply written 'Women' under *Interests and activities*. Some recruiters might possibly find that funny. But the majority probably won't, even those that do certainly won't risk shortlisting such a candidate. Another candidate listed 'Breathing'. Personally, I find that more of a necessity than a hobby.

Case study

Jane has a wide range of activities outside work, and because she's got enough space available, she details her *Interests and activities* in a separate section. And she rounds off her CV with a simple statement about her references.

Interests and activities

Currently include: Badminton, Squash and Pilates
Theatre (local amateur dramatics) and Cinema (especially classic films)

References are available on request

PART 3

THE 15 MOST COMMON CV WRITING MISTAKES

Chapter **14**

How to avoid them!

I have seen many thousands of CVs, covering pretty much every possible type of job, and the differences in them is vast. However, the same common mistakes crop up time and time again. Too many jobseekers miss out on their dream job because of a small number of easily avoided blunders.

Some of the mistakes that people make when writing a CV are very obvious and others are much more subtle. The CV Centre® has conducted a comprehensive analysis of over 2,500 CVs to derive a 'top 15'. In this chapter, I will list the 15 most common CV writing mistakes and refer you back to previous chapters where necessary, both to explain why they are a mistake and also to explain how to avoid them.

1 Inclusion of photographs

People often include photos of themselves on their CV. Don't! Unless you are applying to be a model or wish to work as an actor/actress, then including a photo with/on your CV is definitely not recommended – at least not in the UK.

The whole point of a CV is that the recruiter has a brief, factual description of your abilities, and photographs allow recruiters, rightly or wrongly, to develop a preconceived idea of you as a person, which might well count against you. They may have an irrational aversion to facial hair, for example! An interview is the most appropriate place for the recruiter to first see an applicant, not the CV.

For a longer discussion on the topic of photos, please refer to Chapter 2: Aesthetics and presentation: looking good on paper.

2 Inappropriate heading

Your CV should be headed with your name – and just your name, boldly and clearly before your contact details. It should not be headed 'Curriculum Vitae' or 'CV' or anything else.

Just your name. And only your first name and your last name.

Traditionally, CVs were headed with 'Curriculum Vitae', or suchlike, but this convention is very much on the way out now, which is probably a good thing, given how frequently it is misspelled!

BLOOPER!

One candidate actually headed his CV 'Kuriculam Vitay'!

For further details on how to head your CV, please refer to Chapter 5: Personal details.

3 Missing or inappropriate email addresses

Whilst having no email address at all on your CV is a problem, it's not something I see very often. Far more common is the use of fun or jokey email addresses.

Whilst these may be fine for corresponding with friends and family, employers will probably regard more 'serious' email addresses as more professional.

BLOOPER!

....

You might have the perfect CV, but if your email address is mrluvverman@example.com then it may harm your chances!

I would suggest you open a new email account to use for professional purposes (e.g. Hotmail or Yahoo!) and keep your professional correspondence separate from your personal correspondence.

To learn more about how to handle email addresses, please refer to Chapter 5: Personal details.

4 Superfluous personal details at the top of the CV

My clients often feel that it is compulsory to include details such as their marital status, nationality, number (and ages) of children/dependants. It certainly used to be the norm to include this sort of information on a CV, but it is becoming increasingly rare, given modern anti-discrimination legislation, to find these sorts of details on a CV. They simply aren't relevant.

Too many candidates get too personal. A recruiter does not need to know whether or not you're married, how many children you have, where you like to go on holiday, what your partner's name is or what you normally have for breakfast. These facts should not affect whether or not you can do the job! They simply clutter up your CV, making it harder for recruiters to get to the key information that they really need to see.

I talk about this subject in greater detail in Chapter 5: Personal details.

5 Lack of clear section headings/separation of sections

It is vitally important for your CV to be easy for the reader to scan quickly, so clear section headings and separation of sections is essential. I often recommend the use of lines or other graphic devices in this respect, although there are other ways of achieving a clearer separation.

Issues such as white space, readability and graphics are covered in detail in Chapter 2: Aesthetics and presentation: looking good on paper.

6 Writing in the first person

The words 'I' and 'me' are often used repeatedly in homemade CVs. CVs should be written exclusively in the third person. Making a CV too personal by using 'I' and 'me' tends to look unprofessional. It can convey an impression of arrogance and egocentrism: 'I this ...', 'I that ...', 'I the other ...', 'me, me, me!' But most of all it's just too informal. It might seem unnatural to write a document about you and yet never use either 'I' or 'me', but recruitment experts conclusively agree that this is the best way to do it. Don't give your reader I-strain!

The third person can sound a little stuffy at times but it generally reads better and comes across as more professional. It gives you greater scope to brag about yourself without actually sounding as if you're bragging!

How do you write something in the third person? Take a look at Chapter 3: Content and style: what to say and how to say it.

7 Lack of proper Professional profile and/or Objective

A *Professional profile* is a brief statement at the very beginning of a CV, which, in the space of a few short lines, conveys to readers an overall impression of your key personal and professional characteristics. It's essentially an introduction and should give readers an overview before they read on in further detail.

An *Objective* section explains your preferred career direction and details what you hope to achieve from your future career.

It is very important to include a sufficiently detailed and very carefully phrased *Professional profile*, and, if space permits, *Objective* at the beginning of the CV. The reader needs to know instantly what you're about and what sort of position you are looking for. This is also a key area to consider tailoring for different applications. It's one of the first (and sometimes only) sections the reader will see and consequently gives you a vital opportunity to make a powerful first impression on them.

I tell you how to go about constructing these sections in Chapter 6: Professional profile and Chapter 7: Objective.

8 Inappropriate section order

It's extremely important to choose an appropriate order for the various sections of your CV. For example, the decision whether to put your *Education and qualifications* before or after your *Career history* is critical.

It all depends on what your greater selling point is. You should make sure that all the most important information is conveyed on the first page, or in the top half of one-page CV.

Which do you feel is more likely to be of interest to a prospective employer, your *Education and qualifications* or your *Career history*?

I help you to answer this question in Chapter 4: Structure: which type of CV is right for you?

9 No bullet pointing

In today's fast-paced world, recruiters no longer have the time to read large, solid blocks of prose. They need to extract the information they need quickly. Long paragraphs of text are tiresome for a recruiter to read right through, and many simply won't bother.

And this is where bullet pointing comes in, unfortunately, however, many people fail to use it to their advantage within their CV. Whilst I wouldn't recommend you use bullet pointing everywhere (not in your *Professional profile*, for example), I would very strongly recommend its use in your *Career history*.

I talk more about bullet pointing and the importance of readability in Chapter 2: Aesthetics and presentation: looking good on paper.

10 Reverse chronological order not used

It is a standard convention on CVs to use reverse chronological order, i.e. to present your most recent information first, followed by older and, consequently, less relevant information. And I would strongly suggest you make sure your CV conforms to this.

Many people find this illogical and don't feel comfortable with the idea. But look at it this way:

Should the first job you ever did; for example, working in a pub to support your studies, really be the first thing a prospective employer sees when looking at your *Career history*? If you're now a managing director, it's going to look a tad irrelevant. And when they look at your *Education and qualifications*, what should they read first, details of the GCSEs you sat ten years ago, or details of the MA in Applied Communication that you've just completed?

More about this in Chapter 4: Structure: which type of CV is right for you?

11 Excessive details of interests

You should aim to keep the *Interests and activities* section brief. As with every other aspect of your CV, include what you feel will count in your favour, but be selective about it. Many people write far too much in this section.

No 'Socialising' or 'Clubbing' please, as a recruiter will inevitably imagine you are going to come into work hungover on a regular basis! Even if you do plan to go into work hungover on a regular basis, it's best not to advertise the fact! And best not to risk putting down 'Travel' either (unless you want to work in the travel sector), as a potential employer will inevitably worry that you are about to take a long career break to see the world.

BLOOPER!

• •

Choose carefully. You may indeed have a passion for model railways but do you really want the recruiter to know that?

The *Interests and activities* section of your CV is discussed in much greater detail in Chapter 13: Interests and activities.

12 Date of birth included

I often get asked whether or not you should include your date of birth (or age) on a CV. The old answer to this used to be that you should include it, because recruiters expect to see it and so if you don't include it then it'll just draw attention to the fact.

However, this advice has now changed with the introduction of the Employment Equality (Age) Regulations 2006 (superseded by the Equality Act 2010). And, besides, any recruiter worth his or her salt will be able to deduce pretty accurately exactly how old you are just by looking at your education, qualifications and experience.

There is also a security (identity fraud) risk involved in volunteering this highly personal data to all and sundry. Should your CV fall into the wrong hands, this is precisely the sort of information an identity fraudster needs to clone your identity.

13 Referees included

Details of referees generally shouldn't be included on your CV. They're a waste of valuable space! They clutter it up and, more importantly, you will find that your referees get pestered unnecessarily by time wasters. By the time they have handled their umpteenth enquiry of the day, they are a lot less likely to say nice things about you!

A simple statement at the bottom of your CV saying, 'References are available on request' is more than sufficient because it's not information that a recruiter needs to have up front. When your application progresses to the next level and there is serious talk of a job offer, then that is the time to provide these details.

There are of course exceptions to the rule, and I talk at greater length about the topic of referees in Chapter 12: Other details.

14 Spelling, grammar and typos

STATISTIC

Our research has shown that 60 per cent of the CVs we receive contain linguistic errors.

It is impossible to stress enough how important this issue is. Spelling and grammatical errors are amongst the most irritating errors a recruiter sees, amongst the most damaging errors you can make, and are also amongst the most easily avoided, so check, check and check again, and then have someone else check for good measure!

Just one misplaced letter can make a huge difference to your career prospects. Common errors include candidates stating, for example, that they 'worked closely with the Finance Manger'.

BLOOPER!

In one unfortunate case, the individual got very confused about the difference between 'role' and 'roll'. He kept referring throughout both his CV and his cover letter to the various 'rolls' he had had, e.g. 'an important roll in the finance department', 'sharing a roll with another colleague' etc.

For the full story on spelling, grammar and typos please refer to Chapter 3: Content and style: what to say and how to say it.

15 Length

This is one of the most common problems I see when people prepare their own CVs; they're too long.

I have seen CVs over 30 pages long (true!) with photocopies of all the individuals' certificates on top of that.

This is not an autobiography you're writing. It's a curriculum vitae. It's a lot shorter!

I always advocate a one-page CV if it is feasible, and some recruitment agencies, especially headhunters, may insist on a one-page CV.

Failing that, two pages are entirely acceptable, and, in certain circumstances, it may be acceptable for a CV to run to three or more pages, but only for some senior or technical posts, e.g. medical, engineering.

For a longer discussion about the length of your CV see Chapter 4: Structure: which type of CV is right for you?

For more information on those 'special cases' please see Chapter 16: Special cases – professions where the rules are different.

16 Lack of Achievements section

Yes, I know I said this chapter would cover the 15 most common CV writing mistakes but everyone loves a bonus, don't they?

So here's a 16th mistake for you: failing to include an *Achievements* section.

Including an *Achievements* section will not necessarily be appropriate for everyone but if it could be deemed to be appropriate to your circumstances then I feel it would be a mistake to leave it out.

Please refer to Chapter 11: Achievements, to learn all about the *Achievements* section.

PART 4

WHEN THE USUAL RULES DON'T APPLY

Chapter **15**

Ten solutions for ten potential problems

Everybody is different and every CV is different. Some people's lives and career paths are relatively simple; others are much more complex.

In this chapter I will tackle the ten common and potentially tricky situations in the most positive way possible.

1 What if I have little or no relevant work experience?

2 What if my current job isn't relevant to the job I am now looking for?

3 What if there are gaps in my *Career history*?

4 What if I have changed jobs far more frequently than the average?

5 What if I've been with the same organisation for my entire career?

6 What if I am overqualified for the role for which I am applying?

7 What if I am underqualified for the role for which I am applying?

8 What if I have been dismissed from a previous position?

9 What if I've been made redundant?

10 What if I am worried that my age may count against me?

1 What if I have little or no relevant work experience?

The most common reason for a candidate to lack experience is that they're newly qualified, possibly a recent school leaver or a recent graduate. If this is the case then make the most of what you've got.

You need to lead with your *Education and qualifications* section. This is your biggest selling point and you should give it all the attention it deserves; therefore it should be the most significant feature of your CV.

Immediately after your *Education and qualifications* you should pick out skills you've acquired during your studies at school or university and feature them as bullet points within a *Key skills* section, regardless of whether or not you've yet had a chance to apply them in the workplace.

If your work experience has been intermittent, part-time and principally for the purposes of helping to fund your studies rather than having any relevance to your future career, you should still mention it. Some workplace experience is always better than none.

You can also expand the *Interests and activities* section to include, for example, roles of responsibility you held in societies or clubs, volunteer work etc. Normally this is a section you should keep brief but recent school leavers and graduates are entitled to pad it out just a little bit.

Don't worry if your CV is only one page long; if you have little or no work experience then a recruiter won't be expecting a two-page CV from you.

Another reason for lacking relevant experience is that you have decided to change career path.

2 What if my current job isn't relevant to the job I am now looking for?

If you're trying to change career path then this will be one occasion where you might very well be better served by a functional CV.

You need to declare your future career intentions in an appropriately phrased *Objective*. This will help to avoid any confusion on the part of the reader.

Your previous experience might not be directly relevant but you should still present it in the best possible light. Try to focus on the transferable skills and abilities that you have developed by making use of a *Key skills* section.

You can also dilute any attention which might be focused on your current role by following your *Key skills* section with a *Key experience* section. The *Key experience* section should highlight aspects of your career history that are most relevant to the role you are now looking to undertake.

Your circumstances may be such that you are keen to apply for work in an industry or sector in which you used to work but have departed from in your recent employment history. For example, you could be applying for a job in banking, which you used to work in a few years back, but the more recent experience is in retail.

In this situation I would recommend you contemplate separating out the different types of experience. For example, instead of one section of *Key experience* you could have a section on *Banking experience* followed by one on *Retail experience*.

3 What if there are gaps in my Career history?

Unexplained gaps in your employment record can raise concerns in the minds of recruiters. They may think you have something to hide! And many recruiters will immediately draw their own conclusions (generally not very positive ones) and reject your application.

A useful trick I have already mentioned is to cover up brief chronological gaps by listing only years, not months, within your *Career history*. I'd recommend doing this regardless of whether or not you have any gaps. I consider listing all the months to be unnecessary detail (although some recruiters, especially some recruitment agencies, may still insist on all the months being listed and medical professionals should always provide full details).

It can be problematic if you have larger gaps than can be concealed by simply omitting the months. Most people have a gap or two in their career history. It's very common and not normally anything to worry about.

How you go about handling a gap depends on the reasons for that gap.

If you have a gap as a result of voluntary work, self-employment, free-lance work etc., then it's not really a gap at all and you should see this all as part and parcel of your *Career history*.

However, of the many reasons for gaps within a career history, only one will be viewed favourably by an employer:

➤ Further training/education.

Other common reasons include:

➤ raising a child;

➤ caring for another dependant and

➤ travel.

But there are also reasons which will definitely be viewed negatively, these include:

➤ inability to find a suitable position;

➤ ill health and

➤ imprisonment.

If the reason for the gap isn't obviously negative, then there shouldn't be a gap in your CV; instead, you should include a brief entry explaining the situation.

Further training/education: This is very simple and doesn't really qualify as a gap. Provided you clearly state the dates in both your *Career history* and *Education and qualifications* sections the reader will hopefully be intelligent enough to put two and two together.

Raising a child/caring for another dependant: If you took time out of your career in order to raise a child, or care for another dependant, then it is very much your own private affair. However, it's definitely best to include a brief entry on your CV explaining the circumstances rather than leaving an unexplained gap.

Travel: Taking a sabbatical to go travelling is often (but not always) seen by an employer as a positive thing. Many will believe that the cultural awareness and sense of independence you will have gained as a result of the experience will prove to be of value to them. Also, if you've already taken time out to travel then it means you're less likely to suddenly disappear to travel the world just as they've got you settled in. (This is a common worry amongst employers, particularly when it comes to younger employees.) Include a brief explanation on your CV (and I do mean brief), making reference to any temporary and part-time work you might have undertaken in other countries, if that could be an additional selling point for you.

Unfortunately, general unemployment and ill health are unlikely to be viewed favourably by a recruiter, at least initially. And imprisonment certainly won't be viewed favourably.

My advice is to avoid making an issue of them on your CV. Research shows that less than half of recruiters notice gaps during their initial sift. Rather than try to explain yourself within your CV, thus drawing attention to the issue, you'd be much better off covering such matters at interview. With a bit of luck, the recruiter won't even notice at interview either!

4 What if I have changed jobs far more frequently than the average?

Getting through a large number of jobs in a short period of time can ring alarm bells in recruiters' heads. They may conclude that you are not capable of committing yourself or of maintaining your focus. They may deem you to be fickle. It's a natural enough assumption – even if it's not justified.

BLOOPER!

As one candidate stated on his CV:

Note: please don't misconstrue my 13 different jobs as job-hopping. I have never quit a job.

There may be any number of reasons why you have changed jobs so frequently. Explaining the reasons isn't important; the key is to emphasise what you have learned and what you are now able to offer an employer as a result of this breadth of experience. Highlight the diversity of the organisations you worked for, and the variety of skills which you acquired as a result.

And the best way to communicate this is to use a functional CV.

Implement a *Key skills* section highlighting the transferable skills you have developed during the course of your career: administrative, organisational, interpersonal, skills etc.

You should then proceed to a *Key experience* section, citing specific examples to support what you have said in the *Key skills* section.

And you should conclude with a *Career summary* rather than a full *Career history*.

How do you know what to put in and what to leave out, if you've had lots of work experience?

Include information that's in your favour and leave out information that isn't.

And finally, if you're applying for a permanent role, make it perfectly clear that you are now looking for a permanent role, even if you aren't actually planning to stay for long!

5 What if I've been with the same organisation for my entire career?

There are both positive and negative ways in which a recruiter will view candidates who have worked for the same organisation for the majority of their career. Whilst some people may consider this to be a reflection of commitment and loyalty, others may see it as a sign that the person is not keen on change, or has, for whatever reason, been unable to change.

On balance, I don't feel this to be as much of a problem as some candidates believe it to be. You'd be surprised how many top executives have forged almost all of their careers in one single organisation. In fact, staying with one employer used to be desirable. It's only in recent decades that people's career paths have become much more complicated.

A career is a career, whether you've worked for only one organisation or a dozen. You will no doubt possess a wealth of transferable skills, abilities and experience, and you should make sure your CV communicates this comprehensively. During the course of your career you will most likely have undertaken a variety of roles and each of these should be given the attention they deserve.

TOP TIP

You must be prepared for an interviewer to ask you why you've stayed so long with one single employer, but you shouldn't fear that this fact alone will hold you back in any way.

6 What if I am overqualified for the role for which I am applying?

This is not a common situation but one that certainly does arise, especially in times of higher than average unemployment. Alternatively, you may have decided to take a step back from your career for personal reasons, for example, to achieve a better work–life balance.

Being overqualified for a position is a significant hurdle, as employing such an individual can pose a major risk to an employer. Are you desperate and prepared to take any job going whether you are really interested in it or not? Are you going to be disappointed with the role and move on quickly? Are you going to cause problems in the hierarchy?

You don't want recruiters to be asking themselves these sorts of questions.

The usual rule with CV writing is, 'If you've got it, flaunt it!' However, in this situation, the secret is to downplay your qualifications. Make them less prominent.

If you're overqualified by virtue of your actual academic qualifications then you should make sure that you place your *Career history* before your *Education and qualifications*, moving this discreetly to a second page if possible.

If, on the other hand, you could be seen as being overqualified as a result of your current or most recent employment then, whilst you should adhere to the rule of highlighting skills and experience which are most relevant to the job for which you are applying, you should selectively tone down the scale of your duties and responsibilities.

It's all a matter of getting the pitch right. You're pitching for a particular job, so make sure that your CV reflects this, and won't give the impression that you'd rather be doing a different job. If you fail to convince the reader that you really want this job then you don't stand a chance.

7 What if I am underqualified for the role for which I am applying?

There is really very little point applying for a job if you do not have the required qualifications and experience; it's a waste of your time and the employer's time. For example, if a job advert specifies that the candidate must be highly proficient with MS Access and you only have a basic working knowledge, then there is very little point in applying for the position. You can be absolutely sure that there will be applicants who do fully meet the criteria and you can't compete with them. It's a very competitive job market out there.

However, there are, of course, exceptions.

If you only just fall short of the criteria but feel you have other qualities which will give you an edge, then it may still be worth a shot. It's very much a matter of judgement whether or not you should proceed with your application.

Case study

The advert for the job Jane is applying for stipulates they require:

... a thorough working knowledge of MS Access

Although Jane has little practical experience in its application, she has recently completed a CLAIT qualification and so does have a very good theoretical knowledge. Demonstrating a strong theoretical understanding of a selection criterion, even if you have not yet had the opportunity in practice, is an allowable exception to the normal rule.

To give you another example, a job advert might state that the employer is looking for someone with a minimum of five years' experience and you only have four, but you have an additional and relevant qualification, which is not mentioned in the advert. Look at it from the recruiter's point of view. What is more important to them, the extra year of experience or the additional qualification?

Whilst you should always make the very most of what you've got, unless you have a 'hidden ace' up your sleeve, in terms of your qualifications and experience, you should avoid applying for jobs where you don't comfortably match their criteria.

8 What if I have been dismissed from a previous position?

What if you were sacked for gross misconduct from your previous position (or any position, for that matter)?

I made the point in Chapter 9: Career history that you shouldn't take up valuable room on your CV explaining your reasons for leaving, whether you were dismissed or left of your own accord. That space can be better used incorporating additional sales points.

It is not advisable to include anything in your CV that does not add value or could appear in any way negative. And being sacked for gross misconduct is definitely a negative!

Whilst you shouldn't make any mention of this on your CV, you may still find yourself having to explain the situation at interview. I have two pieces of advice for you on how to handle this:

➤ You must be truthful; it's easy for a prospective employer to check up on this.

➤ Convey the circumstances as calmly and dispassionately as possible, acknowledge responsibility for the causes of your dismissal and, above all else, convince the interviewer that you learned a great deal from the experience and that this will never, ever happen again.

> **BLOOPER!**
> ....
>
> *The company made me a scapegoat, just like my three previous employers.*

9 What if I've been made redundant?

I fully appreciate that redundancy is a difficult time and that there's often little justice in an employer's choice of who to make redundant. I empathise entirely. However, whilst it's unlikely that you've been made redundant through any fault of your own, the fact that you have been made redundant may unfortunately be perceived in a negative way by a prospective employer.

The simplest solution to this is to not make any mention of the fact on your CV. I've already explained that including your reasons for leaving a job is unnecessary, and redundancy is no exception.

The subject may come up in interview, and you must conceal any bitterness and resentment you may feel and, instead, convey to the interviewer that 'such is life', 'these things happen', it wasn't your fault. It is the position that is redundant, not the individual person. Under no circumstances should you criticise the employer that laid you off. Rather than dwell on negative aspects, you must aim to emphasise any positive outcomes; for example, it gave you the opportunity to undertake some valuable training.

10 What if I am worried that my age may count against me?

Your age should not count against you. Various pieces of legislation, notably the Equality Act 2010, are in place to prevent this. However, the reality is that discrimination persists regardless of such legislation and the last thing you want is for your age to be a stumbling block when it comes to getting an interview.

Too many candidates 'over a certain age' see their age as a negative aspect of their CV. Before you even start writing your CV, get this kind of thinking right out of your head. Concentrate on the wealth of experience you have to offer. You've spent a lifetime learning and developing your skills. There's absolutely no justification for someone counting your age against you. William Gladstone was still going strong as British prime minister at the age of 84!

Having got yourself into a more positive frame of mind, let's look at a few practical measures you can take to help counter any possible discrimination.

The best technique is to place the focus very firmly on your most recent history and to radically summarise earlier information. I would suggest splitting your *Career history* into a *Recent career history* section spanning the past decade or so and a *Previous employment* section. You can go into appropriate detail with the former, but the latter should list only job titles, employers' names and locations, no dates or details of duties, responsibilities and achievements.

Your *Career history* will inevitably be more important than your *Education and qualifications* and, therefore, should be listed before your *Education and qualifications*, certainly not after. If your most recent qualifications go back several decades then there's absolutely no need to include the dates within this section. And if your qualifications are limited to O levels passed in the 1960s, then why mention them at all? They have absolutely no relevance to your current employability.

Whilst an *Achievements* section is almost always a welcome addition to a CV, make sure you limit your entries to recent achievements. Don't go back any further than the jobs you've included in your *Recent career history*.

By making it hard to guess your age from your CV, you may arouse some curiosity but that shouldn't reduce your chances of being called for an interview. On the contrary, it has been shown to increase your chances.

Chapter **16**

Special cases – professions where the rules are different

Certain professions and lines of work have specific requirements when it comes to CV writing. Whilst a lot of the advice I give you in *The CV Book* is generic and can be applied to anybody, regardless of their profession, in this chapter I will cover the particular requirements of a number of professions where the rules are somewhat different.

Medical CVs

Although recruitment to medical posts is increasingly conducted via application forms, CVs are still essential for many vacancies.

As a medical professional, you'll possess extensive qualifications following many years of training, and very possibly many years of experience. Your prospective employers will definitely want to know all about this and a medical CV will, therefore, inevitably be longer and more complex than the average CV.

You may possess quite an extensive variety of professional experience, including numerous posts you held for only a short period. As such, your *Career history* should state not only years but also months. You may even decide a functional CV would suit you best.

As well as those in the 'standard' CV, there are a number of other sections that are appropriate for a medical CV:

➤ Clinical skills
➤ Audits
➤ Research
➤ Presentations
➤ Publications
➤ Teaching

TOP TIP

You should aim to order the sections of your CV logically and more or less according to the value they contribute.

As well as providing comprehensive details of your *Education and quali-fications*, it is also important to demonstrate CPD. Yours is a profession where you are expected to be continually learning and much value is placed on CPD by employers.

Medical CVs are an exception when it comes to including information about references. The reader will be expecting full details of your referees right from the start.

You will also be expected to provide details of your professional registration, including reference numbers. These can be listed under *Other details*. But don't include details of your hepatitis B status; it's jumping the gun.

Fitting all this into two pages is a fairly tall order and so it's absolutely fine for your finished CV to run to three, four or even five pages. However, if it starts to exceed five pages then you may be falling into the trap of packing in an excessive amount of information, and this could make it harder for your key selling points to stand out.

For example, whilst it's certainly a good idea to list any research projects, it would be a mistake to provide too much detail. Try to summarise and remain concise. Prospective employers can always ask for further information if they require it, maybe at your interview.

Finally, you should adopt an appropriate tone or voice; a formal, academic style will work best.

Academic and scientific CVs

Academic and scientific CVs have many similarities with medical CVs.

There will be a lot of information that a prospective employer will be expecting you to communicate. However, you must be careful not to provide too much detail, for example, overly long descriptions of projects, excessive technical detail.

You might be itching to write extensive descriptions of the work you've undertaken but it's vital to summarise and stick to the main points. You can always elaborate at your interview, if necessary, but packing too much information into your CV is likely to reduce your chances of winning an interview in the first place.

It may be appropriate to implement additional sections detailing any publications etc. However, the general recommendation for academic and scientific CVs is that they should not exceed two pages – three as an absolute maximum. You have to be concise.

You may need to use specialist terminology to illustrate your points, but, as I have previously pointed out, excessive jargon is not a good idea. If you need to use a specialist/technical term that you are not sure the reader will understand, then it is perfectly acceptable to follow it with a brief definition in brackets.

Teaching CVs

The way you approach writing a teaching CV will depend on the level you've reached in your career. Newly qualified teachers (NQTs) will focus on their qualifications, whereas more senior teachers will focus on their practical experience.

Teaching CVs have a tendency to be longer than the average CV; however, you should still be aiming for a maximum of two pages. You'll normally be backing up your CV with a fairly lengthy cover letter. (Cover letters are particularly important for job applications within the teaching profession.)

TOP TIP

CPD is essential within teaching and should be a prominent feature of your CV, preferably in a separate dedicated section. You could include details of any in-service education and training (INSET) days.

IT skills should be highlighted. They are increasingly important, especially with interactive learning resources now being commonplace.

Extracurricular activities are also of particular interest within teaching. Recruiters will be looking for evidence that you really want to get involved with all aspects of school life, contribute to the community and build relationships with your students both in and out of the classroom.

Legal CVs

Legal CVs don't differ greatly from standard CVs. You still need to keep to a two-page maximum and you still need to ensure your sales pitch is as strong as it can be. However, there are a couple of differences you need to be aware of.

The sheer competitiveness of the sector means that recruiters may want to look at your academic background in great detail. As such, a legal

CV should be very comprehensive in this respect, including full details of institutions attended and grades achieved, at all levels of study.

You should also be very precise when detailing your *Career history*, citing cases of particular importance, significant court results etc. But don't get too bogged down in detail; stick to the key points.

One final word of warning: You should be especially careful not to disclose any information which is legally or commercially sensitive.

IT CVs

IT CVs are frequently very complex, so it's vital to focus on communicating extensive information clearly and concisely, being especially careful in your use of jargon.

You may have worked on a wide variety of different projects and contracts, and, consequently, find that the functional type of CV is most appropriate.

Highlight your specific technical skills in a separate section of your CV, broken down by category. For example:

➤ Hardware

➤ Software

➤ Programming languages

➤ Network protocols

You should also flag up any relevant affiliations, such as membership of the British Computer Society or accreditation with Microsoft, Cisco etc.

If you have a broad range of experience and a high degree of technical proficiency then it is acceptable for your CV to run to three pages. But don't use this additional space to pad out your CV with unnecessary detail.

Engineering CVs

The rules for engineering CVs are very similar to those for IT CVs:

➤ The functional type of CV may be the most appropriate.

➤ You can break down your skills under separate section headings.

➤ Affiliations, memberships and accreditation should be highlighted.

➤ It's acceptable for your CV to run to three pages if necessary.

Architecture and design CVs

If you work within a highly creative and artistic field then a lot of the standard rules of CV design can be thrown out of the window!

Prospective employers will be on the lookout for original thinkers, which will impact on the way you design your CV. They'll be looking for you to demonstrate a bit of flair.

The content of your CV won't be drastically different from the average CV; however, the way it is presented could be.

I won't be giving any design tips; it's your field of expertise. Let your imagination run riot! However, I would warn you not to lose sight of the importance of readability.

Performing arts CVs

As a performer you'll probably be well aware that the CV you need bears little resemblance to a traditional CV.

Issues such as your age (or playing range), height, hair colour, eye colour, ethnicity and frame/build, which would never normally appear on a CV, suddenly take centre stage.

You should also focus the spotlight on that all-important Equity number.

Subsequent sections of the CV could cover your TV, film, theatre, voice-over credits, as well as special skills such as singing, playing the flute, scuba diving, skiing, juggling, languages spoken, accents mastered. You may even wish to include your agent's contact details. But try to keep the finished CV down to one page.

You'll also need to arrange for a winning headshot (choose your photographer carefully if you don't want to bring down the curtain on your career), and you may even decide to print your CV onto the back of your headshot rather than onto a normal sheet of paper.

You've chosen to work in a very challenging sector, and, as with any other sector, a powerful CV can really help you to upstage the competition.

Break a leg!

Military/civilian transition CVs

A career in the armed services is clearly unlike any other. However, for most service personnel a time will come when they wish to return to Civvy Street.

It's a very big change.

You need to remember just how much you have to offer a prospective employer: discipline, courage, motivation, leadership and coaching skills etc. Whilst you might not have much in the way of directly relevant experience, you possess a plethora of highly valued transferable skills which many employers are actively searching for.

The key to successfully writing a military/civilian transition CV is to take off your military cap and start thinking from the point of view of prospective employers. There's much you will have to say about your military career, but try to communicate in terms that a civilian will understand.

It's an excellent idea to include details of awards, honours, volunteer activities etc., but endeavour to keep your readers in mind at all times. What is it that they're really looking for?

A functional CV, firmly focusing on your skills and abilities, is undoubtedly the way to go.

Chapter **17**

CVs and résumés – looking for work abroad

Fashions and accepted norms for CV writing can vary considerably from country to country. In many countries a CV isn't even called a CV; it could be called a résumé or any one of a number of local terms.

In *The CV Book* my focus is very much on the UK. However, in this chapter I will briefly discuss the particular requirements of a small selection of different countries. These are all countries I know to be popular amongst our clients when it comes to living and working abroad.

Most of the basic principles remain the same; however, there are many subtle, but important differences.

Ireland (Éire)

Irish CVs have traditionally been much longer than UK CVs. However, this is steadily changing with more and more employers preferring the standard maximum of two pages.

As Ireland is a bilingual country, language skills are of above average interest to Irish employers. Make sure that you detail the languages you speak in full, including the level (specifying your mother tongue).

The *Interests and activities* section is also particularly popular; you are entitled to elaborate on this section more than you would do in the UK.

A final key difference is the way you handle referees. You can list the details of at least two referees (either one professional and one personal or both your current and previous employers) on a separate sheet. Stating 'References are available on request' is permissible; more and more employers are adapting to the UK style of doing things.

France and French-speaking Belgium

The French use exactly the same term 'CV' that we use in the UK. They don't use *'un résumé'* (at least not in this context).

French CVs tend to include a lot of detail which we now consider superfluous in the UK. Date of birth (or age), nationality, marital status and details of children are all virtually compulsory for French CVs. There's no need to include details of referees, though you can simply state: 'Références disponibles sur demande'.

French CVs are briefer than UK CVs; one-page CVs are a lot more common than in the UK, even for individuals with many years of experience. Two pages is an absolute maximum.

You shouldn't include a *Professional profile*. The *Objective* section is particularly important in France, and they don't just want to know your current objectives; they'll be interested in your career objectives for the next five years.

Including a photograph is popular in France, so it is important to ensure that you have a high-quality passport-size photograph. I'd recommend you consider using a professional photographer rather than an automated booth.

You can attach the photograph to the front of your CV using a paperclip. However, I feel it is more visually impressive to design your CV in such a way as to leave an appropriate space for the photograph (the top right-hand corner) and then carefully glue it in place; this also prevents your photo getting separated and being lost. You should write your name and contact details on the back of the photo – just in case.

One final bit of advice: Always write your last name in BLOCK CAPITALS. It's the way they do things in France.

TOP TIP

Your gender won't necessarily be easy to deduce from your first name. Help foreign employers out by stating clearly, in their language, what your title is; for example, in France 'Mrs' becomes 'Mme'.

Germany, Austria and Switzerland

A German CV isn't a CV or a résumé; it's a 'Lebenslauf' (all nouns are capitalised in German) and should always be of the chronological (reverse chronological) type, not the functional type.

Date of birth, place of birth and nationality are all required details. Marital status is popular but not obligatory.

A photograph is also generally required. You should follow the same guidelines as for France, in this respect.

Unless there's direct relevance to your work, don't include an *Interests and activities* section.

Applying to work for a German organisation can be quite a bureaucratic process! You are likely to be required to provide photocopies of the following documents, if available:

➤ certificates for all formal qualifications gained;

➤ certificates or diplomas for all further training undertaken;

➤ work/residence permit and

➤ driving licence.

It used to be accepted practice to bind all these documents together in a folder. However, a simple staple will now suffice, if there aren't too many pages.

Whilst you may have to submit a lot of accompanying paperwork, the CV itself should be kept a reasonably brief yet comprehensive two pages, listing full details of all qualifications, including grades.

Italy

Comprehensive personal details are expected: date of birth, place of birth, nationality, marital status and details of children. However, as in German-speaking countries, unless there's direct relevance to your work you shouldn't include an *Interests and activities* section.

Apart from that, styles vary widely. I'd recommend you generally follow the UK format and keep your CV down to two pages.

One interesting point is that Italy has very strict privacy laws and it is essential to grant the reader permission to make appropriate use of your CV. You should add the statement: '*Autorizzo il trattamento dei dati personali contenuti nel mio curriculum vitae in base art. 13 del D. Lgs. 196/2003,*' to the bottom of your CV, which means, '*I agree to the use of personal information contained within my CV under Article 13 of Legislative Decree 196/2003.*' This must be followed by your signature.

Spain

As in Italy, comprehensive personal details are expected, right down to your passport or ID card number. It is also very popular to include a photograph.

Unlike Italy, you can include details of your *Interests and activities*.

The United States of America

A CV is of course a 'résumé' in the USA.

The most important difference is the style. Your résumé should be written in a more aggressive style than a UK CV; you really have to sell yourself. The *Objective* section is critical; you need to pitch hard and fast. Try to think like an American!

The functional approach is also very popular, focusing on your key skills and experience – your key selling points. Details such as *Interests and activities* are irrelevant.

Anti-discrimination legislation is just as stringent in the USA as it is in the UK. Therefore, you should exclude all the same personal details you'd exclude in the UK, your date of birth, marital status etc. You should also never include a photograph unless specifically asked to do so.

A résumé preferably only covers a single page, although two pages are acceptable.

And don't forget to use American spelling!

TOP TIP

If you're a European citizen and applying for work outside the EU then it's important to highlight your right to work in the country you are applying to.

Canada

Canada is a country of two languages – English and French. In the English-speaking regions you should adopt the American résumé style of CV. In the French-speaking regions, you should use the French CV style. However, it is worth noting that most Canadians use the term 'résumé' to describe the finished document, regardless of their mother tongue.

Australia and New Zealand

Down Under, they also prefer the term 'résumé'. However, Australian and New Zealand résumés are longer than American ones – typically two to three pages.

They follow the same format as UK CVs except, as they are longer, you will be expected to be more comprehensive.

Details of referees are also commonly included and should be listed at the bottom of your second or third page. It is unlikely, however, to be held against you if you prefer to say, 'References are available on request'.

South Africa

The terms 'résumé' and 'CV' are used interchangeably in South Africa, but both have the same meaning.

It is acceptable for your CV to run to several pages; however, I'd still recommend you aim to be concise and keep to a two-page document.

The style does not differ greatly from the UK CV, but you will be expected to provide your date of birth, place of birth, nationality and marital status.

TOP TIP

If you're based in one country and the prospective employer is based in another country, then you should endeavour to include international dialling codes with your phone numbers.

PART **5**

TAILORING YOUR CV

Chapter **18**

How to adapt your CV for every application

Many people use a general CV designed to suit any position they are applying for; however, greater success can be achieved by tailoring your CV according to the needs of the specific role to which you are applying.

It is astonishing how many people use exactly the same CV for every single application they make.

It stands to reason that every job and every organisation is different, and as such, every CV should also be different, even if the differences are subtle.

I could have discussed tailoring your CV with you earlier in this book, under the relevant chapters. However, I believe you will find it easier to create an initial 'master' CV, which you can then tweak and adapt as necessary rather than starting off by writing your CV with a specific vacancy in mind.

Some people will recommend that you should write your CV virtually from scratch for each and every application you make, but I think you'll agree that there are unfortunately not enough hours in the day! So unless you are considering applying for two (or more) vastly different fields, then having one master CV which can then be easily adapted is the perfect starting point.

Seeing the world from the recruiter's point of view

The recruiter's task is to identify the best matches between the vacancy and the candidates. They're not looking to find you the job that is best suited to you. They're looking to find a candidate that is best suited to their vacancy.

So you need to look at your CV from the recruiter's perspective. Instead of taking your skills and experience as the starting point, your starting point needs to be the requirements of the vacancy.

Too many people fall into the trap of focusing on themselves and not on the needs of the prospective employer. Recruiters are not interested in your life story! They are purely interested in whether or not there is a match between your background and the requirements of the role.

You can even go beyond this and take a closer look at the organisation itself. What sort of organisation is it? What is its ethos? What sort of culture does it have? What type of people does it employ? Why do you want to work for this organisation in particular? Showing an organisation that you would fit into their workplace is a very good habit to get into when tailoring your CV.

HOW TO ADAPT YOUR CV FOR EVERY APPLICATION

> **TOP TIP**
>
> ●●
>
> If all your CVs are the same, then any statements you make are necessarily going to be generalised. What you need to do is carefully relate your skills and experience to those the recruiter is looking for.

Is it really worth the effort?

Many people think this is all too much effort, or are scared that if they tailor their CV to a particular vacancy it might come across to the recruiter as if they've made too much effort to please.

As if it was possible to make too much effort!

On the contrary, surveys show that around a quarter of recruiters will, in fact, give preferential treatment to CVs that they feel have been tailored specifically to the vacancy. In a world where everyone is constantly bombarded with impersonal spam, the fact that you have taken the effort to tailor your application to better suit the vacancy will not go unrewarded.

For every advertised position there will be a considerable amount of competition. The employer could easily have over 100 applications to deal with. If you take a few minutes to tailor your CV (and cover letter) then the odds should increase very much in your favour.

A carefully targeted CV can easily mean the difference between success and failure.

Key words

If you have a job advert or description or person specification then an essential technique is to actually repeat back to them the key words the recruiter has used. For example, let's say their advert states they are looking for:

A creative and innovative individual able to manage their workload on their own initiative

Don't repeat this verbatim straight back to them in your *Professional profile*:

> *A creative and innovative individual, able to manage her workload on her own initiative*

A lot of people fall into this trap!

You should, instead, aim to weave the key words into the overall flow of your CV. This is much more subtle – almost subliminal – but its effect should certainly not be underestimated.

EXAMPLE

A highly creative individual who excelled at university, gaining a 1st class BA (Hons) in Graphic Design. Most recently responsible for managing a heavy caseload on own initiative, liaising directly with clients to develop innovative solutions to their design needs.

By carefully mirroring the recruiter's own use of language you will definitely score points.

Which sections to tailor?

The *Professional profile* and *Objective* sections are obviously ideal places to tailor your CV but you may still need to tweak other areas, such as the descriptions you have given in your *Career history*. For example, the bullet points outlining your responsibilities and achievements in the *Career history* can be reordered to give priority to those which reference skills mentioned in the job advert. You can even remove some points that don't add any value for a particular position.

If you have included a *Key skills* and/or separate *Achievements* section then this might well benefit from some rewriting, or at least reordering, of the points you have raised.

In fact, these are not the only sections that might need tailoring; it all depends on the circumstances. If, for example, you are applying to work for a charity, even if it's not in a hands-on fundraising capacity, e.g. as an administrative assistant, then you might like to expand your *Interests and activities* section so that it highlights some of your charitable interests. Maybe even consider including these as a separate section altogether so that they stand out even more.

Checklist

Here are my top five tips for tailoring your CV effectively:

1 Read the job advert and job description carefully. You can't tailor your CV if you don't actually match the requirements.

2 Keywords are crucial. Make sure your CV reflects the keywords in the job advert. But don't just throw them in without context; otherwise, they become meaningless.

3 Research the company and use your CV to show you would fit into their team.

4 Get someone else to read the CV for you and compare it to the job advert so that they can give you that all-important 'recruiter's perspective'.

5 Don't just change the profile and objective. Look at how your *Career summary* can be restructured to showcase relevant experience.

PART **6**

LINKEDIN

Chapter **19**

LinkedIn

What is LinkedIn?

Many people have still not heard of it and those that have either don't understand what it is for or are still not using it to its full potential.

You will most likely be familiar with Facebook. Facebook is a social networking tool generally limited to social and not professional relationships. But the king of professional and business networking online is LinkedIn. And your first step in networking online should, therefore, be to create a LinkedIn profile.

You need to be aware that (a) LinkedIn is growing at a phenomenal rate (340 million+ members according to recent LinkedIn stats), and becoming an essential part of everyone's job-hunting and networking strategies and (b) that there are many differences between a LinkedIn profile and a CV.

Never seen LinkedIn? Have a look at my LinkedIn profile and you'll see what I mean: **www.linkedin.com/in/jamesinnes**

It's important to get a good balance when writing your LinkedIn profile; to get the right 'angle' and the right 'tone'. You need to be professional and yet still reveal a bit of personality. You also need to be careful of using the right keywords so that your profile succeeds in the search results.

So why is LinkedIn so important?

LinkedIn has now become one of the most important websites both for recruiters searching for potential candidates and for people trying to find a new job. It's also invaluable for keeping up with the latest developments in your industry and for making new connections.

So, why is LinkedIn so important?

LinkedIn gives you the opportunity to connect with a company or a person within that company directly like never before. Recruiters are actively recruiting via LinkedIn and they could well be looking for you, so you had better stand out from the crowd.

If you already have a profile, let's do a quick LinkedIn audit. If you don't have a profile as yet, take a note of what's important.

Your photo

Is your photo recent? This is one of the first things that a recruiter will see on LinkedIn and having a good photo that you use across all networks says something about you. It says that you are professional and care about your public image. A professional head-shot is best, ideally against a plain background and not in a pub with friends!

Customising your LinkedIn URL

Have you claimed your public profile URL? Claim your public profile URL so you can promote your profile in your CV, email signature, business card, blog etc., in an attractive, memorable and easy-to-read format.

The headline

Is your professional headline up to date? The LinkedIn headline is a maximum of just 120 characters long (including spaces), but because it sits directly underneath your name on the profile page, it is vitally important. Along with your photo, it helps to create the right first impression and to attract attention. Your headline needs to say so much more than just your current job title. It should succinctly say what you are all about, what your main area of expertise is and what value you can add to a company.

Adding industry-specific keywords to your headline is important, but with just 120 characters you can't get carried away so choose carefully. Don't go for generic buzzwords that recruiters see all the time but for words that make you stand out.

Here are some examples of LinkedIn headlines that could grab the attention of recruiters:

PRINCE2 qualified Project Manager with 12+ years' experience managing the full SDLC for blue-chip clients

Internationally experienced HR Director | recruitment & retention specialist | strategic advisor at executive level

Senior Sales Manager who substantially increases profits by developing strong client relationships

Writing a LinkedIn summary

Is your summary relevant? If your summary is no good then recruiters won't even take a look at the rest of your profile.

As the first detailed section of your LinkedIn profile, the summary is where you can really sell yourself to potential recruiters. It is vitally important and should never be left empty! Unlike the profile at the top of your CV, this should be written in the first person and should aim to expand on what you wrote in the headline.

If you are using LinkedIn to find a job, the summary is a good place to include a 'call to action'. Remind recruiters of your email address so that they can contact you easily and tell them what you can do to add value to their company. Even if you just want to use LinkedIn to expand your contacts network, this is where you can impress other people with your skills and expertise by showcasing your career achievements.

The summary on LinkedIn has a limit of 2,000 characters, which is quite a lot! I wouldn't recommend using all of this. Just as recruiters only spend a maximum of up to 30 seconds looking at your CV, they may spend even less time scanning your LinkedIn profile. So keep it brief and make every word count.

Examples of some statements that will make your LinkedIn summary really stand out:

As a manager of business critical software development projects with over 12 years' experience, I have been instrumental in delivering value-adding solutions to clients in diverse industry sectors from pharmaceuticals to logistics. Whether managing a project from inception or being called in to take over a struggling project, I am renowned for always delivering on time and within budget.

My philosophy in life, both personally and professionally, is to make the very most out of every opportunity you are presented with. In the workplace, this has translated into leveraging maximum possible value from all client interactions, winning numerous company-wide awards for my outstanding performance against targets.

Making the most of your experience

Is your experience current? Just like your CV, it's important to keep LinkedIn up to date at all times.

Use your experience section to give credence to the skills you have highlighted in your headline and summary. LinkedIn is all about connecting with people, so you need to stand out. To do this, you need to demonstrate your accomplishments. Use stats and results where appropriate, but be careful not to share confidential company information in this very public space. Also, if you have been promoted within a company, make sure your readers can see this.

Remember what you are using LinkedIn for and make sure that this is reflected in your experience section. If you are targeting a particular job or a particular company, highlight the most relevant information from your past experiences. Engage with your audience by keeping them interested.

For each of your job roles, you have a maximum of 2,000 characters. As with the summary, this is very generous and I would recommend you keep it brief.

Structuring your experience section to highlight achievements is trickier on LinkedIn as it doesn't support the use of normal bullet points. But you can just use a hyphen instead and get the same effect as demonstrated in the example below:

Managing an extensive portfolio of blue chip clients, I am responsible for all aspects of account management with the emphasis on improving the client experience whilst simultaneously driving profitable growth.

Key achievements include:

- *Negotiating a lucrative 3-year contract extension with Blue Chip Company worth over £2 million*
- *Transforming an underperforming account into a profitable partnership by improving communication and strengthening relationships*

Add media

In the Summary, Education and Experience sections of your LinkedIn profile, you have the option to upload a document, photo, link, video or presentation to help you to showcase your greatest achievements visually. This is an incredibly effective way of making your profile stand out from the crowd and also gives recruiters the opportunity to learn even more about you. In the text-heavy world of LinkedIn, this can make a real difference.

Skills and endorsements

There is space on your LinkedIn profile for you to add up to 50 skills and your connections can then endorse you for these skills. Choose skills that are reflected in your experience section so they are more likely to be endorsed by your colleagues or clients. Also, choose skills that are key-words for the industry or job role that you are targeting to help recruiters to find you. The skills with the most endorsements will be listed first on your profile.

And remember, a good way to encourage other people to endorse your skills is to endorse theirs!

Recommendations

Do you have more recommendations than you have given out? That's a good sign that you are a well-liked and reliable individual. Get as many recommendations as you can!

You can wait for colleagues, managers, clients or business partners to recommend you, but you can also be proactive about this. LinkedIn gives you the option of asking your connections for recommendations. A default message can be sent out but it is better if you customize this to make it more interesting and personal.

LinkedIn recommendations can be hidden if you don't think they are adding any value to your profile. You can even ask for them to be revised if they don't say quite what you expected.

As with endorsements, don't forget to give recommendations to other people; it may result in a recommendation of your own!

Additional sections

The most important sections that you need to complete on LinkedIn have already been covered but there are plenty of other sections that I would encourage you to complete if you can. These include Publications, Projects, Volunteering Experience, Organizations, Education, Honors & Awards, Interests, Courses and Certifications. Showing recruiters what your achievements and interests are outside of the workplace can give them a real insight into your personality. If you are targeting a particular company, try to ensure that these reflect the values of that company so that they can see you will be a perfect fit.

Once you have populated all the sections you can, feel free to change the order that they appear on your profile so that the most important ones are seen first by recruiters.

Things to think about

Have you imported your email contacts? Import all your email contacts to make sure your email acquaintances are also your LinkedIn connections.

Have you customized your email invitations? 'I'd like to add you to my professional network on LinkedIn' is the standard message everyone receives. Change it and stand out!

Have you joined relevant groups? Join relevant groups, post relevant articles and participate in discussions to connect with major players in your industry by using the search tool to find groups by industry.

Once you have completed your LinkedIn profile, the last thing you want is to lose all that information if the website experiences data losses. So you have the option to download and save your profile as a PDF. It's always good to have this as a backup. You can even download the profiles of your connections in the same way!

LinkedIn keyword research

A recruiter searching for the right candidate on LinkedIn (or Google for that matter) is going to use certain keywords. You, therefore, need to be aware that everything in your headline, skills section, experience and summary needs to be full of the keywords that recruiters are likely to be looking for.

You probably know some words that should be associated with roles you want, e.g. marketing, executive, manager, creative, account-ant, sales. But you need to appreciate that there are a lot more keywords surrounding these words that different people will search.

One great way of doing this is to use **www.wordle.net** as follows:

➤ Find a few job postings for the kind of jobs you are looking for.

➤ Copy and paste them all into Wordle to see instantly which are the most commonly used keywords within the job listings.

➤ Ensure these keywords are covered in your current job title, status, your summary and your experience.

And, finally, but very importantly, remember to insert an email address, and preferably, also a phone number into your profile so you can be contacted more easily once they've found you!

How to build your LinkedIn network

If you add just the people you know already on LinkedIn, chances are you won't get much beyond 100 connections. However, I believe that, in most cases, you should expand your network to its maximum. The further your reach, the greater exposure you have to opportunities.

You have to be careful about adding the right people. If too many people click 'I don't know this person', in response to your invitation, then there's a risk that LinkedIn will delete your profile without any warning. Clearly best avoided!

Try to get to 500 connections as quickly as possible and then be more strategic about who you add.

Besides importing all your current connections, you should search under 'TopLinked' for groups and then request to join them. When you have been accepted (it takes about a week) then you'll be able to download a 'CSV' file. You can then invite people and they will accept you with no questions asked.

Having a large network also means that you'll be able to connect with more people through second- and third-degree connections.

You can still be successful by only connecting with people you know; it's just that it can be a little tougher in the long run. It all depends on what you want to get out of LinkedIn.

How to stand out from the crowd and get noticed

Show your worth.

Join groups and answer questions. This is great for your personal brand as it gives you the opportunity to show off how much of an expert you are in certain subjects. LinkedIn recommends groups that it thinks you may like based on the information in your profile. But you can also search for groups in the directory by using keywords.

Contribute to groups with as much value as possible and think about starting your own group. It's a great way to add value to LinkedIn. Once you have joined in some discussions with the group, and begun to engage with other group members, you can invite them to connect with you. Then you can see what they are up to and try to be of service.

Just as you would with other social media sites such as Facebook, keep your activity feed on LinkedIn up to date with regular posts. Share information and resources that your connections might find interesting and let them know of any developments in your own career. Also, any updates that your connections make to their own profile will be shown on your activity feed, so keep an eye on these. Show an interest by liking their comments or by leaving a response.

Identify and connect with recruiters. What is your target market? Identify who could recruit you. Who can make that decision? You first need to know what companies you want to work for. Then you need to find out who is hiring at the company. Check what groups they or their close connections are active in. Who has influence on that person? Perhaps it is the founder of the company if they are an SME. The goal is then to position yourself and persuade the hiring manager to hire you. Do not try adding them before offering them some value.

The best way to connect is to find out what keeps them up at night. What is going on in the industry that you could help with? With groups you can do this. The default setting on LinkedIn is that if you join a group, you allow other members of that group to contact you. Also, in groups, you'll find job postings relevant to that group.

I don't believe in a set email to send to recruiters when you first contact them. Check out their profile and see if they recommend a way to contact them, and remember to be personal. The main priority when sending that initial message is not to be too pushy. Tell them that you have been researching the company and express your interest in the possibility of working with them, outlining what it is that you have to offer them.

Remember: You must have a perfect profile before connecting with people you want to work for!

How to find a new job without your current employer finding out

You may not want your current employer knowing that you are using LinkedIn to find a new job. So use the Privacy & Settings menu to toggle your activity broadcasts. That way, whenever you change your profile, make recommendations or follow a company, this information will not be shared in your activity feed.

Promoting your LinkedIn profile

The more people who know about your LinkedIn profile, the more visitors you will get. In turn, this could result in increased connections. If you have a Facebook profile, or a Twitter account, make sure they include a custom URL for your LinkedIn profile. Also, add this to your CV and to your email signature.

Upgrading your membership

There are a number of paid-for membership options giving access to some of the additional features LinkedIn has to offer. Whilst most people will find the free membership perfectly fine for their needs, some recruiters and job seekers may benefit from upgrading to a premium account. All of these memberships offer a free 30-day trial before you commit to paying a monthly fee, which currently ranges from £19.99 to £79.95.

Key features of premium accounts include the ability to see who has viewed your profile recently, unlimited profile searches, advanced search facilities and in-mail messaging to contact anyone on LinkedIn even if you are not connected.

My top ten tips for LinkedIn

Here are my top ten tips for LinkedIn:

1 Write job descriptions for each position. Packing your job descriptions with carefully chosen keywords is incredibly important if you want people to find you. They also need to know what you did in your last job.

2 Complete the skills and endorsements section. This section allows you to list key skills and knowledge areas. Keywords are crucial.

3   Create a personal URL. When a recruiter or potential client researches you, you want them to find compelling and positive information. By creating your personal LinkedIn URL recruiters will find you easily.

4   Make your profile public. You shouldn't be hiding your profile from potential recruiters. To change this, click on the 'edit profile' tab and look for 'Public Profile'. Click the 'edit' next to the URL and you will arrive at the page where you can choose what to make public.

5   Add a decent photo. Not having a photo is a bad idea and so is having a poor photo. Make sure it looks professional.

6   Have your profile proofread before putting it live. Just as with your CV, you can't afford to have errors on your LinkedIn profile.

7   Personalise the 'invitation to connect' message. LinkedIn is a social network, so be social! Don't be like everyone else and use the standard text.

8   Use company profiles as a research tool. Company profiles provide so much useful research information. Follow companies you are most interested in working for.

9   Don't promote yourself too heavily in LinkedIn groups. Nobody likes to be spammed. Be useful, not annoying.

10 Check out the LinkedIn Jobs tab. Remember that LinkedIn lists a lot of jobs, so keep an eye on them!

Professional LinkedIn profile writing

If you would like one of The CV Centre®'s team to help you with your LinkedIn profile, then just visit our website for further details:
www.CVCentre.co.uk

PART 7

LOOKING AT THE WHOLE PICTURE

Chapter **20**

Cover letters

According to a recent survey, almost 50 per cent of recruiters think cover letters as being just as important as the CV, although most people spend the least amount of time on them.

Many people lose out on an interview because of their cover letter. People tend to blame their CV without giving a thought to their cover letter, yet it's frequently the cover letter that is to blame for the lack of success.

Never underestimate the importance of a cover letter

The cover letter sets the tone of the application and should inspire the reader to turn over and read the accompanying CV.

It is the ideal opportunity for you to succinctly summarise and re-emphasise the skills and experiences you have highlighted in your CV, whilst also giving you greater latitude to express your personality. It can help to focus attention on your strengths and distract attention away from any weaker points.

Get it wrong and you may find that the recruiter doesn't even bother to read your CV. Applications can be rejected solely on the quality of the cover letter, so I would strongly recommend you take your time in preparing your cover letter and maximise your chances of getting through to the interview stage.

The 15 most common cover letter mistakes – and how to avoid them!

The CV Centre® has conducted a comprehensive analysis of over 1,000 cover letters to derive a 'Top 15' of the common mistakes people make.

1 Failing to write to the right person

The best person to address your cover letter to is the person who is going to be making the decision whether or not to interview you. Too many letters are simply addressed to the 'HR Manager' and start, 'Dear Sir/ Madam'. You want to try to get right through to the decision maker. This is an elementary sales tactic, but unless you work within sales, you're unlikely to be aware of how important it is to reach the person who actually has the power to make the decision you want them to make.

2 Not including your full contact details

I would recommend that you start all your letters with a professional-looking letterhead. It is vital that the reader can quickly spot your name and how to get in contact with you. Put your name at the very top, followed by your address, phone numbers and email address. Place your address on one line with your phone numbers on the next and finish with your email address. It's exactly the same as your CV.

3 Inappropriate email addresses

Fun or jokey email addresses are fine for corresponding with friends and family; however, employers will regard more 'serious' email addresses as more professional.

You might have taken time to put together a brilliant cover letter, but if your email address is mistressdominatrix@example.com then it may harm your chances!

4 Losing the reader's interest with your opening words

The primary goal of your opening paragraph is to explain to the reader why it is that you are writing to them.

Yes, you're applying for a job – they'll figure that out pretty quickly. But why are you applying for this job? If you fail to start building your case immediately you risk losing the reader's interest right from the very start.

5 Not saying what job you're applying for

At the beginning of your letter you should always clearly state the position you are applying for along with any reference number(s) quoted in the job advert. It is very possible that recruiters will be simultaneously seeking candidates for various positions, and it will make their life a lot easier if they can clearly see which vacancy the letter refers to.

6 Failing to make your case

Whilst it would definitely be a mistake to arrogantly oversell yourself, it is also a mistake to undersell yourself. Don't be afraid to blow your own trumpet and show a little self-confidence in what it is that you have to offer a prospective employer. It's a tight job market out there. You need to compete effectively if you're to stand any chance of achieving your career goals.

Make sure you give them compelling reasons to invite you for an interview.

7 Repeating what's written in your CV

Too many people fall into the trap of repeating the majority of what is in their CV. This will not only weaken the impact of the letter but may even put a recruiter off reading the CV.

A cover letter is an opportunity to draw the reader's attention to some of your key selling points – skills, experience, achievements – and to do so in a way which makes it clear how these will be of interest and potential benefit to the reader.

They've got a copy of your CV. Your cover letter should complement it, not repeat it. Your cover letter should introduce your CV, not replace it.

8 Lack of 'call to action'

Make sure you end your letter in a positive, upbeat manner. You can't demand a response from them but you need to do everything in your power to encourage one.

This is where a little advertising device known as a 'call to action' comes in handy.

'Call to action' is a term used in advertising to describe a message to readers of an advert or other promotional material, which is specifically designed to motivate them to take some specific action, perhaps pick up the phone and place an order, for example, 'Call now whilst stocks last!'

You need to devise something similar to close your letter.

9 Talking about money before you've even got your foot in the door

You should never voluntarily bring up the subject of money in an initial cover letter. It can be a fatal mistake because it sends a clear message to the reader that you are more focused on your own needs than you are on theirs.

10 Giving the reader I-strain

The word 'I' is often overused in cover letters. Unlike a CV, a cover letter should be written in the first person. However, if you start every sentence with 'I' then it can make for pretty tedious reading.

It might not be easy to cut down on your use of 'I' but you should definitely make an effort to do so. Look at each sentence which begins with 'I' and see if you can rephrase it so that it starts with 'You' or 'Your', this is ideal because it shows your focus is on the reader, not on yourself.

11 Lack of coherent structure

Like all the best stories, the best letters have a strong and clearly defined beginning, middle and end. It's important to make sure that your letter is structured in a logical fashion. Capture their attention, make an impact, maintain their interest and finish with a strong closing paragraph.

You've only got a certain amount of space and a certain number of words to get your message across. If you don't structure your letter carefully then you'll end up rambling, and the impact of your letter will be severely diluted.

12 Length

As a general rule, most cover letters shouldn't exceed one A4 page in length. Never lose sight of the fact that your cover letter is not intended to take the place of your CV; it's meant to act as an introduction.

Unless there are clear instructions to the contrary, you should aim to keep your letters short and succinct. Two to three paragraphs is normally more than sufficient to whet the recruiter's appetite and entice them to read your CV.

13 Spelling and grammatical errors

It might seem hard to believe that people actually send out letters with errors in them. But, believe me, it happens all the time, so if you can make sure that your letters are totally error free then you will immediately be at an advantage.

It is essential to double-check that there aren't any spelling or grammatical errors. This is most likely the recruiter's first impression of you. Make sure it's a positive one.

14 Spamming everyone with the same letter

In just the same way that a CV should be tailored for each application, so too should a cover letter. In fact, it is even more important to tailor a letter. A carefully targeted letter can mean the difference between success and failure.

It stands to reason that every job and every organisation is different; therefore, every CV and every cover letter should also be subtly different. If you send the same letter to everyone, changing only a few minor details such as name and address, then your chances of success will most definitely fall considerably.

15 Not signing the letter

Whilst you won't be able to physically sign a letter sent by email, you should always sign letters sent by post.

By taking the time to sign the letter before sending it, you're giving out one further signal to the reader that you have taken the time to write to them personally and haven't just sent out the same letter to dozens of people.

My five top tips to make your cover letter stand out

Make an effort to accommodate these five points when writing your cover letter and you'll immediately be well above average.

1 Get through to the right person

The best person to address your cover letter to is the person who is going to be making the decision whether or not to interview you. Not only do letters addressed to a specific person achieve better results, but letters that actually reach the decision maker have an even higher chance of making the grade.

2 Communicate clearly, concisely, engagingly and articulately

It is essential for your letter to be easy for the reader to scan quickly and effectively. Take your time to carefully phrase your thoughts; do not rush. Make sure you get your message across.

3 Tell a good story

Like all the best stories, the best letters have a strong and clearly defined beginning, middle and end. It's important to make sure your letter is structured in a logical fashion. Capture the reader's attention, make an impact, maintain their interest and finish with a strong closing paragraph.

4 Target/tailor your letter

You should always tailor your letters according to the specific organisation to which you are applying. A carefully targeted letter can easily mean the difference between success and failure. Nobody likes being spammed.

5 Check your spelling and your grammar

Before sending off any letter, make sure you have read through it very carefully and that there are no spelling or grammatical errors. It's always a good idea to ask someone else to double-check it for you.

The Cover Letter Book

If you would like to learn more about cover letters then please take a look at my best-selling book on the subject, *The Cover Letter Book: How to Write a Winning Cover Letter That Really Gets Noticed*. You can place your order for a copy via our website: **www.jamesinn.es**

Chapter **21**

Interviews

Your application has been successful and you have been invited for interview; what next? Some people think they can just turn up and be themselves, which is fine, but it won't get them the job! You need to work hard to prepare for an interview, as you are still up against many other applicants and this is your key opportunity to make an impact.

Planning, preparation and organisation: a winning strategy

The best person for the job, in terms of the right skills, experience and achievements, doesn't always pass the interview and doesn't always get the job. Sometimes the most able candidates on paper can really shoot themselves in the foot when they get to the interview.

The interview is one of the most critical points in the job search process. Whilst you might look great on paper, you need to subsequently prove that to a hiring manager. Many other factors that are not related to the person's ability to do the job are going to be picked up in the interview.

You've got the skills; now you need to demonstrate clearly that you'll be a good fit with your future co-workers and employer, and it's so easy to sabotage this valuable opportunity if you're unprepared.

On average, there are likely to be at least five other candidates being interviewed for the same vacancy. So, everything else being equal, that gives you a 20 per cent chance of getting the job. But there's so much you can do to improve your odds of success.

Pre-interview questionnaire

In order to help you plan and prepare for your interview I have developed the following brief questionnaire. It should help to get you thinking about the most important issues you need to consider.

1 Regarding you and your interview history:
   (a) How many interviews have you attended within the past two years and how many of these have resulted in a job offer?
   (b) If any of your interviews failed to win you a job offer, why do you think that was?
   (c) What, if any, feedback have you received from an interviewer after an interview?

2 If you have won an interview for a specific role within a specific organisation:

   (a) Have you applied for a position at this organisation before and/or what previous knowledge or experience of the organisation do you have?

   (b) What is it about this particular position that appeals to you?

   (c) If this position marks a change in career direction for you then why have you decided to make this change?

   (d) What, if any, is your understanding/perception of the organisation's internal culture?

   (e) What, if any, further information do you have with regard to the kind of skills and experience the organisation is looking for?

   (f) Have you been asked to prepare a presentation, and, if so, what instructions have you been given? For example, content, time, visual aids to use.

Interview scenarios: expect the unexpected

There are many different types of interview. Here are some of the possible scenarios with which you might be faced:

- Classic one-on-one interviews
- Panel interviews
- Competency-based interviews
- Psychometric and aptitude tests
- Presentations
- Group interviews
- Assessment centres
- Telephone, video-conferencing and webcams

Interview questions: and their answers!

Whilst there are thousands of possible questions you could be asked, it's important you prepare thoroughly for the following 'top ten'.

You should make sure you think very carefully about your answers to all these questions before getting anywhere near an interview room. Try to understand the meaning behind each question; what the interviewer's intentions are in asking you the question.

1 Tell me about your work experience – what did you do, what did you enjoy, what were you good at, why did you leave each job?

2 Why have you applied for this vacancy?

3 Why do you wish to leave your current position?

4 Why do you want to work for this organisation?

5 What are your strengths?

6 What are your weaknesses?

7 What has been your greatest achievement in your personal life as well as in your career?

8 What can you, above all the other applicants, bring to this job?

9 Where do you see yourself in five years' time?

10 You've mentioned x under the *Interests and activities* on your CV. Can you tell me a bit more about that?

You are absolutely certain to get asked at least some of these questions (or variations of them), if not the whole lot.

I could add an eleventh question to the list: 'And do you have any questions for me/us?' There aren't many interviews that conclude without this question being asked, so you'll need to make sure you think of some good questions to ask the interviewer.

My five top tips to interview success

Make an effort to accommodate the following and you'll immediately be well above average.

1 Be prepared

The key to preventing pre-interview jitters is preparation. If you are to be able to convince a recruiter that you are right for the role then you need to get it clear in your own mind why you are right for the role. As well as researching the job, you should also research the organisation.

2 Work through my pre-interview questionnaire

I would recommend you take the time to complete the short list of key questions above before any interview; it should really help to get you thinking in the right direction.

3 Make sure you're there on time

Late arrival is consistently one of the very top reasons cited by recruiters for their rejecting candidates at the interview stage. Don't be late. Better than that, aim to get there early so as to have time to relax and compose yourself.

4 Be confident and show your enthusiasm

Confident people inspire confidence in others; if you appear confident that you are able to do the job, the employer is likely to be more inclined to believe that you can. A lack of enthusiasm is generally fatal to your chances of success. Be enthusiastic – and show it. Confidence and enthusiasm are traits that are guaranteed to impress an interviewer.

5 Don't recite your answers parrot-fashion

It's essential for you to create your own answers to potential questions. Too many candidates make the mistake of sounding like they're reciting answers from an interview book. Even if you have prepared and memorised your own answers, you should make sure that your delivery is natural and doesn't come across as rehearsed.

The Interview Book

If you would like to learn more about interviews then please take a look at my best-selling book on the subject, *The Interview Book: How to Prepare and Perform at Your Best in Any Interview*. You can place your order for a copy via our website: **www.jamesinn.es**

I have also written a best-selling companion volume, *The Interview Question & Answer Book: How to Be Ready to Answer the 155 Toughest Interview Questions*. You can order this book via our website: **www.jamesinn.es**

Chapter **22**

Your new job

This is it! There's no turning back now. It's time to bite the bullet!

In this chapter we're going to deal with how to successfully get through that all-important first day in your new job.

Your very first day in a new job may not be the most difficult you ever face in that job, but you can be sure that it will be packed full of challenges. And what are you going to do? Well, you're going to rise to those challenges, of course!

Setting off

On the morning of your first day, make sure that you allow yourself enough time to get ready (gather your thoughts, go to the lavatory, check your appearance in the mirror etc.). And make sure you know where you're going!

Arriving late on your first day will reflect very badly on you, and it happens all too often. You're most likely going to the same place you went to for your interview but that could easily have been a month or two ago and your memory might be hazy. You need to check precisely where it is that you are expected to go and then make doubly sure that you know exactly how to get there and on time, preferably early!

Into the spotlight

TOP TIP

You are on show from the moment you arrive at your new employer's premises, so try not to look like you've just arrived at the dentist for some root canal treatment!

Your first day is a lot like one long interview. Yes, you've already got the job, but people will be keeping a very close eye on you until you've settled in. And you may have an initial trial period to complete before you can really start to feel secure in your new job. There's undeniably a lot at stake, but it's definitely no cause for panic.

Depending on the size and type of the organisation, you may have to present yourself to reception on the morning of your first day, or your new boss might be there to greet you personally. If the first person you see is the receptionist, be polite and charming; receptionists can have a surprising amount of influence in an organisation, principally because they know absolutely everyone.

When your new boss does turn up, look happy to see them and shake hands firmly, but not to the extent that they end up in plaster! Seriously, shake someone's hand too firmly and they might think you're trying just a little bit too hard. And if you deliver a weak handshake people often think that implies a lack of character.

Whether you feel confident or not, make sure you look it. You might feel like you're back to your first day at school – a little lost. But remember, confident people inspire confidence in others; if you appear confident that you are able to do the job, everyone around you is likely to be more inclined to believe that you can. It's human nature.

Whilst confidence is critical, it is important not to go to the other extreme and appear overconfident or arrogant. That won't go down well at all with your new workmates. Strike a happy balance.

First impressions count

Before you get close to doing any actual work, the first thing you'll be doing is meeting and greeting, and first impressions are extremely important. Everyone you meet today will be making initial judgements about you, and often on the basis of just a few minutes spent together. Sounds scary? It's not really. It's what you do naturally every day when you meet new people, when you go to a party, for example, or out for dinner with friends of friends. So don't put yourself under too much pressure. But do be conscious of the impression you'll be making on others.

Make a poor first impression and you might not be able to recover from it. How quickly do you sum up someone you've just met? It's probably just a couple of minutes. Make sure that you make a powerful first impression on everyone you meet today. Start your new relationships off on a positive foot. Start as you mean to go on.

TOP TIP

Remember: You never get a second chance to make a first impression!

Start new working relationships

Your relationships with the people you work with are immediately going to become the centre of your working life. Building relationships is vital in the workplace. Getting to know your colleagues is one of the most important parts of starting a new job.

But it's too early to get into any great detail just yet; you're only just starting to meet these people.

In these early stages the most important thing to bear in mind is to take the time to meet people and to make the effort to get to know them. First off, you need to ask for and then remember people's names. (Write them down if it helps!) You need to find out more about them; start building up a mental file on them.

Avoid talking about yourself too much; other people prefer to talk about themselves; what you say could later be used against you by the office gossips. Be friendly but remain professional. These people are your colleagues, not your friends.

Keep your ears open. Start building up a picture of the various different characters you'll be dealing with and how they interrelate with each other, listening to what they say and how they behave. You should also note the way that your boss interacts with and manages your colleagues, and the way they react with their peers and their seniors.

Whether you're shy or not, don't be unapproachable; don't be a loner. Get all your new relationships off to an excellent start. It can be tiring and emotionally draining being friendly all day, but make sure you maintain your level of enthusiasm.

The little things count too, like saying, 'Good morning,' and asking how people are. It's surprising how important these little everyday interactions can be. Don't neglect them.

Smile and the world smiles with you

I'm not about to suggest you traipse around all day grinning like a lunatic, but never underestimate the importance of smiling!

Smile at someone and chances are they will smile back. Try it. It's a built-in reflex that we humans have, enabling us to immediately communicate our friendly and peaceful intentions – even at a distance. It's such an innate behaviour that even if you sit by yourself and smile, you'll actually feel better for it! If you don't believe me then try it!

Start with a big smile for your new boss (without looking too smarmy), and then keep a small smile lingering around your lips the rest of the day. It will definitely have a positive effect on the perception that others have of you (firmly proved by psychologists) and you will even feel more positive yourself.

Nerves and anxiety

Nerves can often be a useful tool for sharpening your performance. However, if your nerves take over to the extent that they interfere with your ability to function, then it's clearly a problem.

Nerves are commonly caused by having lots of negative thoughts rattling around your brain. Try to relax, calm your anxious mind and think positive thoughts. Remember: Everyone – and I do mean everyone – gets nervous about their first day in a new job. It's perfectly normal.

Of course, the better prepared you are, the less likely you are to feel panicky, but you'll never completely eliminate nerves. The secret is to channel your nervous energy and use it to your advantage. Take a deep breath, focus, concentrate and don't let nerves spoil your day.

> **TOP TIP**
>
> You will always feel more nervous than you actually look. Bear this in mind and it should help you to calm down.

Not putting your foot in it

It is very important to come across as open and friendly with the people you meet, but keep your guard up. You don't know anything about these people; you don't know their backgrounds, their opinions, their characters; you don't know their relationships with each other. So think before you speak. Steer clear of saying anything too personal or anything which could be remotely controversial or which could potentially cause offence to anyone. Tact is the word. Stick to small talk. It can be all too easy to say something which you might later come to regret. Remember: EBBOM …
Engage brain before opening mouth!

BLOOPER!

· ·

My wife made the big mistake of casually confiding to a colleague that she thought her new boss was 'a bit of a bulldog'. It took less than 24 hours for the boss to find out that their new nickname was 'The Bulldog'!

STATISTIC

· ·

It's not just what you say that can count against you. Surveys show that one of the most common errors a new starter can make is accidentally using someone else's coffee cup! People can be terribly territorial.

Bon appétit

Lunch might just be a quick sandwich at your desk, or if you're a shift worker, lunch might not exist at all. In many workplaces, staff often get together for lunch and there's probably even more chance of this happening if it's your first day. There will be at least one person keen to take the new boy or girl under their wing. And that's when you really have to watch what you say! Lunchtime is prime time for gossip and office politics. Don't be antisocial, but play it carefully.

You could turn down the invitation to have lunch because you have to go to the gym or have some shopping to do or just want to get well away from everyone to clear your head! But be very wary of snubbing anyone on your first day; your first invitation might well turn out to be your last.

Of course, you might not feel much like eating (that's your nerves getting the better of you), but you definitely want to avoid a long afternoon with an empty stomach. Having lunch will:

➤ Boost your energy levels and help you to think straight;

➤ Settle any butterflies in your stomach/acid indigestion;

➤ Stop your stomach from gurgling embarrassingly!

The calm after the storm

After a busy morning when you were very much the centre of attention, you could well find that the afternoon is a calmer affair. Your new boss will probably have run out of people to introduce you to and things to show to you and will hopefully just leave you in peace to settle in.

Seize the opportunity to start getting your workspace organised; throwing out those half-chewed biros that your predecessor left behind, and start reading through the inevitable pile of paperwork that will have been dumped on you. There may even be some helpful handover notes left by your predecessor.

You'll probably find it a useful exercise to write up some notes covering all that you've had to learn and take on board so far today. For example, if you're anything like me – I have a very poor memory for names and faces – then you might well want to jot down the names of the people you've met, along with brief descriptions. You can also start preparing a list of gaps in your knowledge and any questions you have.

TOP TIP

Your brain's probably feeling a little scrambled and it'd be a good idea to 'download' as much information as possible onto paper for future reference.

This should all keep you pretty busy for the duration of the afternoon but you never know, you might find some time to do some real work. Even if you don't feel you're achieving very much, it's not a great cause of concern; nobody is going to be expecting you to work miracles on your very first day.

Time for tea

It varies from workplace to workplace, but pretty much everywhere I've ever worked, tea and coffee drinking have been important tasks. If you're feeling brave then getting up and offering to make or fetch a round of tea or coffee can make a really excellent impression. It might not seem like much but it's a personal gesture which others can hardly fail to appreciate. If you are in doubt as to how the coffee machine works then don't be afraid to ask a co-worker to show you the ropes. Regardless of whether you're on the bottom rung of the career ladder or at management level, you're showing others that you're one of the team and that you're happy to muck in.

Final impressions count too

So, it's time to go home. You're probably pretty tired by now but in just a few minutes you'll be out of the building and away. But, before you go, make sure you politely bid everyone goodnight, smile and leave with your head held high. First impressions are important, but so are final impressions.

There's a chance you might get asked to join a colleague or two for an after-work drink. If you've got enough energy left then a drink might help you to further develop budding new relationships, but you'd be wise to limit it to just a couple of drinks! You've had a long hard day with much to absorb and assimilate and you're probably not up to capping it off with a long night out.

When you finally get home, it's entirely normal to spend most of the evening thinking back over your first day and pondering on things you could have said or done differently. But don't beat yourself up too much; there's no doubt that you will be more sensitive to any possible slip-ups than anyone else was. Try to get some rest, give yourself a pat on the back and remember that tomorrow is another day!

Ultimate New Job

If you would like to learn more about how to get off to the right start in your new job, not only surviving but actually thriving, then please take a look at my best-selling book on the subject, *Ultimate New Job*. You can place your order for a copy via our website: **www.jamesinn.es**

PART **8**

CV AND COVER LETTER EXAMPLES AND TEMPLATES

Chapter **23**

Twenty-one CV examples to help you write yours

This chapter contains a selection of example CVs, which should help to illustrate all the points made in this book, and which should also help you to generate lots of useful ideas for your CV.

I start with the finished CV from our case study, Jane Bloggs, and then cover a variety of different professions, careers, sectors and circumstances.

These examples are based on real-life CVs, which have helped my clients to win interviews; however, most of the details have been changed to preserve their anonymity. In several cases, I have blended together several CVs to better demonstrate key principles. These CVs don't represent real people and real careers, but they do represent the presentation, content, structure and style you should be aiming for when writing your CV.

Free templates

These examples include lots of formatting, which might make it hard to copy directly from this book, or at the very least rather time consuming to do so. Therefore, I have provided a special link for you to go online and download a full set of CV and cover letter templates. There's no charge for this. All readers of *The CV Book* are entitled to this entirely for free.

Simply visit our website to quickly and easily download your free templates: **www.jamesinn.es**

JANE BLOGGS

1 Any Road, Anytown AN1 1CV
Telephone: 01632 960 960 (home); 07700 900 900 (mobile)
Email: janebloggs@example.com

Professional profile

A positive, proactive and results-driven sales manager with a proven track record of profitable business growth through the creation of successful sales and marketing strategies. Experienced in working with leading brands in the competitive food and drink sector, focusing on exceeding customer service expectations, ensuring optimum brand impact. Possesses excellent interpersonal, communication and negotiation skills and the ability to develop and maintain mutually beneficial relationships with key decision makers.

Objective

Having successfully completed a BA (Hons) in Marketing and Advertising, now looking to return to the food and drink sector in a suitably challenging role. Keen to make best use of broad sales experience and strong theoretical knowledge of marketing and advertising.

Career summary

2007–date   Sales Manager, ABC Stationery plc, London

- Playing a key role within a large stationery retailer, tasked with the redevelopment of the sales strategy across the UK market
- Planning and executing innovative campaigns, including direct mail and telesales
- Personally cold calling to bring on board high profile – and credit-worthy – new clients
- Liaising extensively with clients to agree product specifications, sale prices and lead times
- Building mutually beneficial relationships with suppliers, negotiating terms and discounts
- Interviewing, recruiting, training and mentoring new sales executives into the business
- Setting budgets and forecasting sales whilst maintaining full P&L accountability

Key Achievements
- Boosted regional sales levels by nearly 35% over a 2-year period with no additional marketing spend
- Organised a successful new product launch, gaining a substantial amount of local and national press coverage
- Featured in the programme 'Business Lunch' on XYZ TV, providing invaluable exposure for the business

2001–2007   Sales Executive, XYZ Food plc, London

- Primarily tasked with account management, working closely with a small number of key clients
- Successfully pitching new products and lines, providing advice on effective visual merchandising
- Travelling extensively to meet with clients and help devise new strategies for boosting sales levels
- Actively responsible for financial issues such as credit control and resolution of bad debts

Key Achievements
- Led the introduction of a major culture change in customer service, improving customer satisfaction ratings from 6.2 out of 10 to 8.3 out of 10

Page 1 of 2

Career summary cont.

1997–2001   **Marketing Assistant, MNO Drinks plc, London**

- Gaining valuable first experience of sales and marketing within a market-leading plc
- Assisting the Marketing Manager in the development of new campaigns and strategies
- Additionally liaising with external agencies and brand development consultants

Education and qualifications

BA (Hons):   Marketing and Advertising, University of Sussex (2009)
3 A levels: English, English Literature and French (1997)
10 GCSEs: Including English and Mathematics (1995)

Further skills

IT Skills: MS Office including PowerPoint & Access, QuarkXPress and PhotoShop
Languages: Fluent French; basic German

Further training

- CLAIT Level 1: Including optional unit in Database Manipulation (2009)
- Commercial Awareness & Marketing Intelligence (2007)

Other details

Driving Licence: Full/Clean
Health: Excellent; non-smoker

Interests and activities

Currently include: Badminton, Squash and Pilates
Theatre (local amateur dramatics) and Cinema (especially classic films)

References are available on request

Hannah Singh

1 Any Road, Anytown AN1 1CV
Telephone: 07700 900 389
Email: hannahsingh@example.com

Professional profile

A highly qualified MBA student with a unique combination of skills and capabilities acquired during studies and work experience. Able to demonstrate strong customer focus combined with a proven commitment to the achievement of targets and business objectives. Works effectively on own initiative with the organisation and time management required to complete assignments on time and to the required quality standard. Enjoys being part of a successful and productive team and thrives in highly pressurised and challenging working environments.

Objective

Currently looking to secure a marketing internship within a forward thinking organisation, one that will make best use of existing skills and experience whilst enabling further personal and professional development.

Education and qualifications

MBA: Masters in Business Administration (Graduate October 2009)
MASTA London School of Business (accredited by University of Scotland)

MSc: Biotechnology (2007)
Paramedical College, Whalgar University, Calcutta, India

BSc: Biotechnology, Chemistry and Zoology (2005)
Kanpur University, Kanpur, India

Intermediate: Physics, Chemistry, Biology, English and Computer Science (2002)

High School: Mathematics, Science, Social Science, English and Hindi (2000)

Further skills

I.T. Proficiency: Word, Excel, C++, Internet and Email
Languages: Fluent English and Hindi; currently learning French

Work experience

2007–2009   **Customer Care Officer, Pensions R Us Ltd**
- Providing information and advice to employees of several major US hotel chains regarding their pensions plans
- Advising on the availability of suitable pension plans and assisting with the transfer of plans from one fund to another

Interests and activities

Currently include: Photography, Drawing, Reading (autobiographies and science journals), Swimming, Football and Badminton

References are available on request

Hannah Florence

1 Any Road, Anytown AN1 1CV
Telephone: 01632 960 227 (Home); 07700 900 956 (Mobile)
Email: hannahflorence@example.com

PROFESSIONAL PROFILE

An enthusiastic and versatile professional, with strong practical experience in nursing practice within a multi-disciplinary environment and an acute surgical setting, specialising in emergency, elective bowel surgery and vascular surgery. A focused and proactive person adopting a motivated and positive approach to all tasks, with a commitment to deliver the highest standards of patient care at all times. Possesses excellent interpersonal and communication skills with the ability to adapt to any situation and prioritise tasks. Key assets are strong attention to detail, the ability to communicate with patients, families and staff at all levels and a natural facility to work under pressure.

EDUCATION AND QUALIFICATIONS

2009:	VAC-KCI Wound Management
	ALERT
	Immediate Life Support
2008:	Diploma in Adult Nursing
	Adult Protection
2003:	8 GCSEs (including English and Mathematics)

PROFESSIONAL TRAINING

- Intravenous Administration
- Fresenius Volumetric and Syringe Pumps

- Setting up PCAs
- PICC and Central Venous Catheter Use

CAREER SUMMARY

2008–date   *Staff Nurse, Curie Ward – Royal Hampshire Hospital*

- Assessing patient care needs and the development, implementation and evaluation of care programmes
- Assisting in the systematic monitoring and evaluation of nursing practice and implementing standards of patient care supported by solid evidence-based results
- Ensuring all nursing practices comply with the Trust's Nursing policies and procedures including the NMC Code of Conduct, maintaining the highest possible standards
- Developing and maintaining strong working relationships with health care staff, medical staff and other members of the primary care and social services teams in order to deliver outstanding patient care
- Managing a small case-load of patients and coordinating and monitoring individual patients progress along their critical trail
- Actively supporting the implementation and maintenance of Team Nursing within the clinical area and organising patient discharges
- Ensuring all matters regarding the implementation of clinical governance are addressed on the unit including the regular maintenance and evaluation of care standards
- Providing a prompt and appropriate response to complex enquiries and complaints from staff, patients and members of the public in order to prevent any formal complaints
- Responsible for intermittently acting as the 'nurse in charge' under the direct supervision of a senior staff member and coordinating shifts and appropriately deploying staff in line with Trust Guidelines
- Conducting regular ward audits and maintaining an adequate supply of all required equipment and linen in the absence of the Ward Manager

INTERESTS AND ACTIVITIES

Currently include: Reading, Swimming and Dog Walking & Training

REFERENCES ARE AVAILABLE ON REQUEST

Richard Vermont
1 Any Road, Anytown AN1 1CV
Telephone: 07700 900 629
Email: richardvermont@example.com

PROFESSIONAL PROFILE

A dedicated and compassionate medical professional who specialises in the field of spinal neurosurgery. Able to demonstrate strong clinical expertise with the proven ability to assess and investigate patient symptoms and make appropriate decisions on the most appropriate treatment accordingly. Committed to the field of research and development with the aim of improving standards of medical practice through the use of technological advances. A valuable member, and leader, of a successful multi-disciplinary team who thrives in highly pressurised and challenging working environments.

EDUCATION AND QUALIFICATIONS

2006:	Doctorate of Medicine in Neurosurgery, University of Jamaica
	European Final Board Examination in Neurosurgery – Jordan Diploma & Prize
2005:	European Primary Board Examination in Neurosurgery
2004:	Final Intercollegiate Fellowship in Neurosurgery
	Fellow of the Royal College of Surgeons of England
2000:	Doctor of Medicine Part I, University of Jamaica
1996:	MBBS with Honours, University of Jamaica

AFFILIATIONS

- General Medical Council UK (9727294)
- Medical Council of Jamaica (9264)
- Educational Commission for Foreign Medical Graduates, USA (1-934-423-2)
- Member of the Society of British Neurological Surgeons
- Member of the European Association of Neurosurgical Societies
- Fellow of the Royal College of Surgeons of England
- Fellow of the Caribbean College of Surgeons
- Member of the British Medical Association
- Member of the Jamaica Medical Doctors Association
- Member of the Medical Association of Jamaica

PROFESSIONAL DEVELOPMENT

- IELTS
- Communication Skills Course
- OSCE Examiner Workshop
- Epidemiology Workshop
- Advanced Trauma Life Support Certification
- Advanced Cardiac Life Support Certification

- Ultrasonic Aspirator
- Tissue Vaporizer
- Basic Life Support Certification
- Advanced International Microsurgical Anatomy Course
- Advanced Pneumatic Instrumentation Medtronic Midas Rex
- Leeds Spine Study Day

ACHIEVEMENTS

- VIP Pelican, University of Jamaica – Alumni Magazine (2008)
- Jordan Prize for Best Performance in Final European Board Examination in Neurosurgery, Luxembourg (2007)
- Second Place in the European Primary Board Examination in Neurosurgery, Finland (2006)
- Best Performance in the Doctor of Medicine in Surgery Part 1 Examination (2000)
- Jolbury Prize in Medicine for Best Performance in Medicine and Therapeutics in the final MBBS Exam (1996)
- Pfizer Clinical Medicine Award for Best Performance in the Clinical Station in Medicine (1996)
- David Bleak Prize in Anatomy, First Stage MBBS Exam (1993)

CONSULTANT APPOINTMENTS

- The Einstein Memorial Hospital (2006)
- The Lisa Institute of Medical Sciences (2006)
- The University Hospital of Jamaica – Honorary (2006)

CAREER SUMMARY

Current   **THE ESSEX NEUROLOGICAL CENTRE, EXETER GENERAL HOSPITAL**
Locum Consultant Spinal Surgeon – Department of Neurosciences
- Playing a pivotal role in the development of the spinal service at the Exeter General Hospital whilst setting up research and audits relevant to the specific area of practice
- Participating in the on-call emergency rotas for both neurosurgical and spinal as well as conducting routine outpatient clinics, special A&E clinics for semi-urgent referrals and outreach clinics to local district general hospitals
- Managing a full day operating list whilst also attending weekly spinal MTD meetings and departmental governance meetings
- Providing advice and specialist services to local GPs and other medical professionals as well as supervising neurosurgical trainees

2008   **THE SIMPSON CENTRE FOR NEUROLOGY & NEUROSURGERY**
Senior Spinal Fellow
- Conducting pre-operative and post-operative assessment of in-patients and out-patients before assisting with operations both independently and under supervision of the Consultant
- Building rapport with adult and paediatric patients and their relatives and ensuring their full understanding of the neurosurgical conditions
- Playing a key role as second-in-line within a multi-disciplinary team with responsibility for the supervision of junior staff, registrars and ST trainees
- Adopting a collaborative approach to patient care by working in close conjunction with nursing, physiotherapy and occupational therapy staff
- Additionally liaising with neuroanaesthetic, neuroradiology, neurology and neuropathology colleagues regarding the conditions affecting patients
- Participating in a 24/7 on-call service covering adult patients at the Simpson Centre and paediatric emergencies at the Royal Manchester Children's Hospital
- Handling on-call referrals from Doctors in district hospitals and GPs, assessing the clinical details and radiological imaging and discussing the patient with the Consultant before making a decision on the next course of action
- Admitting patients when required and informing Bed Managers of the level of priority for each particular patient
- Playing a key role as Spinal Fellow at the Royal Leeds University Hospital with full involvement in adult operations
- Responsible for teaching junior neurosurgical trainees and medical students to facilitate their professional development
- Attending weekly MDT meetings for spinal surgery, radiology and oncology and participating in clinical audits and research

05/2005–06/2006   **UNIVERSITY HOSPITAL OF JAMAICA**
Senior Registrar – Neurosurgery

03/2003–04/2005   **SLOUGH GENERAL INFIRMARY**
Senior Registrar / Registrar – Neurosurgery

01/2003–02/2003   **UNIVERSITY HOSPITAL OF JAMAICA**
Registrar – Neurosurgery

TEACHING EXPERIENCE

Teaching
- Lecturer, Leeds University (Pending Appointment)
- Lecturer, Faculty of Medical Sciences, University of Jamaica (2006–2008)
- Teaching neuroscience, neuroanatomy, neurology, neurosurgery to medical students, surgical trainees, junior residents, SHOs, postgraduate residents and nursing staff
- Personally requested by the Dean of the Faculty of Medical Sciences to teach neuroanatomy to second year medical students in the Department of Basic Medical Sciences, University of Jamaica

Examining
- Examiner for the Accident & Emergency Nurses Training Programme, University Hospital of Jamaica (2006)
- Examiner for Second Year Physiotherapy Students, University Hospital of Jamaica
- Examiner for Second and Third Year Medical Students in Anatomy, University Hospital of Jamaica
- OSCE Examiner for the University of Manchester Medical Students

RESEARCH AND PROJECTS

Fields of Research
- Neuromicrosurgical Anatomy; Microsurgical Anatomy Lab; Hydrocephalus; Surgical Oncology

Externally Funded Projects
- Acquisition of a New Midas Rex Drill from Medtronic, valued at $30,000 (2001)
- $3,000 grant from Codman, Johnson & Johnson towards the development of the surgical residents group
- Medtronic and Carl Zeiss sponsorship ($15,000) of an International Microsurgical Anatomy course conducted by Professor Jane Sampson (2004)

Publications
- *The Management of Spinal Dural Arterio-Venous Fistulas at The Simpson Centre 2000–2007* (Pending)
- Management of malignant metastatic spinal cord compression – *British Journal of Neurosurgery* (2009)
- Pure subdural haemorrhage from a ruptured PCOM Aneurysm – commentary *WIMJ* (2004)

Presentations
- *Endoscopic Third Ventriculostomy* – Caribbean Neuroscience Symposium, Lisa (2004)
- *Approaches to the Anterior Cervical Spine* – Caribbean Neuroscience Symposium, Lisa (2003)
- *C-Section at the University Hospital of Jamaica – Too Few or Too Many?* – Second Medical Faculty Research Day Conference (1994)

Operative Videos Recorded, Edited and Produced
- Craniotomy and clipping of Left Middle cerebral artery aneurysm
- Clipping of a giant basilar superior cerebellar artery aneurysm via a half and half approach
- Craniotomy and clipping of a PCOM aneurysm
- Craniotomy and clipping of a Rt MCA aneurysm
- Endoscopic third ventriculostomy
- Bifrontal craniotomy and resection of craniopharyngioma
- RT Fronto-temporor-orbital craniotomy and resection of craniopharyngioma
- Transsphenoidal resection of pituitary adenoma
- Endoscopically assisted resection of pituitary adenoma
- Lumbar microdiscectomy L4/5
- Frontal craniotomy and transcortical resection of a SEGA tumour
- Endoscopic third ventriculostomy for posterior fossa tumour
- Endoscopic third ventriculostomy for suprasellar cyst
- Endoscopic third ventriculostomy for post fossa tumour
- Endoscopic third ventriculostomy for post fossa colonic metastasis
- Post fossa craniotomy and resection of medulloblastoma
- Post fossa craniotomy and resection of astrocytoma
- Insertion of syringo-peritoneal shunt for trauma associated syrinx
- Insertion of syringo-peritoneal shunt for tumour associated syrinx
- Craniocervical decompression for chiari 1 malformation without syrinx
- Craniocervical decompression for chiari 1 malformation with syrinx
- Anterior cervical decompression for cervical spondylotic myelopathy
- Orbito-zygomatic craniotomy, pit adenoma and frontal astrocytoma – composite video of image guided surgery at the UHWI
- Clipping of PCOM aneurysm
- Craniotomy & resection of temporal AVM
- Craniotomy & clipping of MCA and ACOM aneurysm
- Craniotomy and clipping of PICA aneurysm
- Craniotomy and resection of Colloid cyst
- Occipital–transtentorial resection of a pineal region astrocytoma
- Endoscopic third ventriculostomy for post fossa ependymoma
- Endoscopic third ventriculostomy for pineal region metastasis
- Anterior cervical microdiscectomy and plating

Development Projects
- Participating in the development of a surgical laboratory at the University Hospital of Jamaica
- Developing a website for the surgical residents groups at the University Hospital of Jamaica

CONFERENCES AND TRAINING

- SBNS Meeting
- European Association of Neurosurgical Societies
- Specialist Fellowship Exam Course
- OSCE Workshop
- Second Caribbean Neuroscience Conference
- First Leeds Aneurysm Surgery Course
- Minimally Invasive Courses
- Inaugural Caribbean Neuroscience Symposium
- Biostatics Workshop
- Ena Thomas Symposium
- Medical Association of Jamaica Conferences
- Biostatistics Seminar
- Temporal Bone Dissection Course

- Microsurgical Anatomy
- Peripheral Nerve Course
- Brain Mapping Course
- Skull Base Approaches
- Endoscopic Pituitary Course
- Microsurgical Anatomy
- Traatek Instrument Training
- Dr Ruth's Microsurgical Anatomy Course
- Minimal Approaches to the Lumbar Spine
- Midas Rex Course
- Society of British Neurosurgical Surgeons
- American Association of Neurological Surgeons
- Congress of Neurological Surgeons USA

FURTHER SKILLS

I.T. Proficiency: Word, Excel, PhotoStudio, Movie Maker, MGI VideoWave Movie Creator and I-photo
Languages: Basic French and Spanish

PERSONAL DETAILS

Driving Licence: Full/Clean
Interests include: Football, Cricket, Athletics, Theatre, Photography, Video Editing and Production

REFERENCES

Mr Paul van Hille

Consultant Neurosurgeon

The Walford Centre
Manchester
UK

Mr Philip von Halle

Consultant Neurosurgeon

Bradford General Infirmary
Bradford
UK

Mr James Holness

Consultant Neurosurgeon

Bradford General Infirmary
Bradford
UK

Mr Albert Infield

Consultant Neurosurgeon

Bradford General Infirmary
Bradford
UK

Professor Albert Johnson

Neurosurgeon

Haptassie University
Canada

Professor Derek Billmore

Neurosurgeon

University of Miami
Miami, Florida
USA

ESTA MORRIS

1 Any Road, Anytown AN1 1CV
Telephone: 07700 900 362
Email: estamorris@example.com

PROFESSIONAL PROFILE

A resourceful, hard-working and dedicated Electronics Engineer and Physical Scientist with an outstanding academic background, a good publication record and significant experience in the design and development of digital and analogue circuits, PLC circuit programming, UHF and HF radars and optical imaging equipment. Possesses excellent presentation skills and can prepare comprehensive documentation and reports as required. Experienced in data processing, is quick to grasp new ideas, technologies and concepts, and is skilled in a range of industry-standard software packages. Works well both independently and as part of a team, demonstrating the motivation and organisation required to meet demanding targets. Combines an analytical and professional approach with excellent interpersonal skills and can communicate concisely at all levels.

OBJECTIVE

Now looking for a new and challenging position, one that will make best use of existing skills and experience and provide opportunity for further responsibility and professional development.

CAREER SUMMARY

2007–date   *Postdoctoral Research Assistant, University of Reading*

- Undertaking enzyme engineering, including cloning, mutagenesis, fermentation, expression, purification and characterisation
- Developing a novel expression system to increase the productivity of Putidaredoxin Reductase ten-fold and transferring the entire production procedure to a commercial basis
- Synthesising fine chemicals by biotransformation using recombinant cells with cytochrome P450 enzymes
- Producing a dehydrogenase end-point reaction platform for further development into a biochemical analysis kit
- Development of electrochemical biosensors for total cholesterol, HDL and total triglycerides, including optimisation of HDL chemistry and development of an immuno-sensor combined with EMIT, writing assay protocols and carrying out protein modification, lyophilisation, immunoassay and ELISA

2002–2005   *Research Assistant, Department of Communications Systems, Basingstoke University*

- Undertaking programming and ensuring the effective operation of UHF radars and HF transmitters in remote sensing research
- Carrying out detailed and cutting-edge signal and image processing activities in order to investigate HF-induced artificial auroras

Page 1 of 2

EDUCATION AND QUALIFICATIONS

2002–2006:   PhD, Space Plasma Environment and Radio Science
               Thesis 'Radio and Optical Observations of Natural and Artificially
               Stimulated Geo-space Plasmas'

1996–2001:   BSc Electronics/Communications Engineering
               Modules include Electrical Circuits, Electronics, Logic Circuits, Control
               Systems and Automation, Telecommunication Theory and Circuits,
               Electromagnetism, Antennas, Microwave Circuits
               Final Year Project 'Design and construction of wireless multi-channel
               handsets for voice and data communication'

AWARDS

Royal Astronomical Society prize for best presentation in National Astronomy Meeting
(2009)

TECHNICAL SKILLS

- *Fermentation engineering*
- *Bioanalysis development*
- *Biosensor Development*
- *PCR, UV/VIS, SDS-PAGE*
- *AUTOLAB*
- *Enzyme engineering*
- *Biosynthesis development*
- *HPLC, FPLC, GC, MS*
- *EMIT, ELISA*
- *Lyophilisation*

PUBLICATIONS

E.A. Bentley, Y. Astier, E. Morris, S.G. Bell, L.L. Wong and H.A.O. Hill. *Inorgania Chimica* 2005; 356 (347–348)

E. Morris, C. Yili, Z. Hechun and W. Wu. Purification and Properties of Cholesterol Oxidase from Brevibacterium. 3rd Symposium for National Young Microbiologist. Wuxi, China. May 29, 2004

E. Morris, C. Yili, Z. Hechun and W. Wu. Colorimetric Determination of the Activity of Cholesterol Oxidase. University of Light Industry. 2003

E. Morris, C. Yili, and W. Wu. Properties of Cholesterol Oxidase from Brevibacterium. The 4th International Conference of Food Science and Technology, Wuxi, China. 2004; 10 (79–80)

PERSONAL DETAILS

Driving Licence: Full/Clean
Health: Excellent; non-smoker
Work Permit: Full UK work permit

REFERENCES ARE AVAILABLE UPON REQUEST

Amanda Whittle

1 Any Road, Anytown AN1 1CV
Telephone: 01632 960 828 (Home); 07700 900 219 (Mobile)
Email: amandawhittle@example.com

PROFESSIONAL PROFILE

An enthusiastic and dedicated legal graduate who enjoys being part of a successful and productive team. A confident and articulate communicator with a professional manner and the ability to conduct impressive and persuasive presentations and work of the highest quality. Extremely organised and highly self-motivated, with a proven background in achieving targets and meeting tight deadlines, performing well in a highly pressurised working environment. Possessing excellent interpersonal and liaison skills with the ability to communicate professionally with customers and encourage colleagues, building and maintaining productive working relationships.

OBJECTIVE

Now looking for a new and challenging position in legal profession that will make best use of existing skills and academic achievements enabling further personal and professional development.

EDUCATION AND QUALIFICATIONS

LLM: **Business and Commercial Law** – *Result Pending*
       2011–2012
         Julius Jenkins University, Manchester
         Modules:

➢ Business and Social Organisations	➢ Corporate Governance
➢ Employment Law	➢ ADR
➢ Commercial Leases	➢ Commercial Contracting

LLB (Hons):   **Law** – *2:1*
       2008–2011
         Julius Jenkins University, Manchester
         Modules:

➢ Public International Law	➢ Family Law
➢ Succession Law	➢ Employment Law
➢ United Nations International Security Law	➢ Financial Crime
➢ Land Law	➢ Equity & Trusts
➢ Obligations B (Contract and Tort)	➢ EU Procedural Law
➢ Introduction to Business Organisations	➢ Property Offences
➢ Introduction to Employment Law	➢ Criminal Law
➢ Obligations A (Contract and Tort)	➢ Public Law
➢ Foundations	➢ Legal Research

Diploma: **Law** – *2:1*
       2006–2008
         Intercollege, Nicosia-Cyprus
         Modules:

➢ English Composition	➢ Basic Writing
➢ Criminal Law I-II	➢ Microcomputer Applications
➢ English Legal System I-II	➢ Contract Law I-II

EDUCATION AND QUALIFICATIONS cont.

High School: Prianpancy Lyceum Larnaca (Cyprus)
  2003–2006
        Modules:
        - ➤ Classical Greek
        - ➤ Latin
        - ➤ Philosophy
        - ➤ French

        - ➤ Modern Greek
        - ➤ History
        - ➤ English

FURTHER SKILLS

IT Proficiency: Working knowledge of Windows 98/2000/XP/Vista
                         Expert knowledge of MS Office 98/200/XP/2003/2007
Languages: Greek (native) and English (fluent)

WORK EXPERIENCE

2010–2012   Part-time Teacher – *Manchester's Greek School*
- Financially supported studies offering comprehensive teaching service to students of Manchester's Greek School including devising innovative lesson plans and teaching strategies
- Gaining experience of effective time and manpower management, addressing queries and issues raised by parents and students and liaising with fellow staff members

2007–2008   Bar Staff – *Grand National, Aintree Racecourse*
- Dynamic and multifaceted role providing professional customer services in sale of food and beverages to patrons
- Developed excellent interpersonal and communication skills interacting with staff and customers remaining affable and focused at all times
- Worked as part of a team to coordinate bar duties in prompt, effective manner

2006–2009   Assistant – *Marathon Tours, Larnaca, Cyprus*
- Offered assistance and gained experience within tourism industry dealing with general enquiries and general administration including ticketing and invoicing

PERSONAL DETAILS

Driving Licence: Full/clean
Health: Excellent; non-smoker
Sports Interests: Prior member of High School Basketball Team, three times Cyprus Champions;   Represented Cyprus in World Championship in Turkey and Hellenic Championship
General Interests: Fashion, Cooking and Dance
Specialised Interests: Vice-Chairperson for two years and then Chairperson of the Greek–Cypriot Society between 2008–2012
                         Participation in Youth Exchange Seminar for European Union in Italy, Portugal, Poland, Greece, Hungary and Cyprus

REFERENCES ARE AVAILABLE ON REQUEST

Robert Ward

1 Any Road, Anytown AN1 1CV
Telephone: 01632 960 238
Email: robertward@example.com

PROFESSIONAL PROFILE

A versatile and dynamic professional with a successful background delivering substantial improvements in standards of teaching and learning. A competent strategist with the proven ability to influence policy and developments to enable a direct impact on children's education. Possesses excellent interpersonal, communication and negotiation skills and the ability to develop mutually beneficial partnerships both internally and externally. A motivational and inspirational leader capable of coaching and empowering teaching staff to enable them to fulfil their potential whilst ensuring that they make a positive contribution to the achievement of objectives.

CAREER SUMMARY

2006-date   **SPECIALIST SCHOOLING TRUST, LONDON**
                    Designation Management Coordinator

- Managing the dedicated team of 11 staff responsible for advising schools on designation and re-designation as specialist schools with a budget of £3.5 million
- Establishing and maintaining mutually beneficial relationships with DCSF, TDA and YST including working with DCSF regarding policy decisions for specialist schools
- Playing a pivotal role in the formulation of new policies, the preparation of bids and the management of £400k of commercial activities
- Producing comprehensive on-line guidance documents for schools as well as creating professional development courses and delivering the same to middle leaders
- Preparing and delivering highly effective presentations to senior staff in schools across the country whilst also presenting seminars to school governors

Key Achievements
- Actively involved in a major change initiative to the re-designation process involving informing schools, training staff and providing feedback to DCSF

1996-2006   **ORANGEMORE COLLEGE, PORTSMOUTH**

2000-2006   **Assistant Principal / Vice Principal**
- Fully accountable for Curriculum Development within the school and for driving improvements in teaching and learning whilst controlling the annual budget of £400k
- Playing a lead role in encouraging the strategic utilisation of ICT within all areas of the curriculum
- Providing management and support to Assistant Principals and Advanced Skills Teachers and contributing to their professional development

Key Achievements
- Personally responsible for the management of three successful re-designation bids for specialist status whilst also successfully achieving Training School status
- Winning numerous grant awards and sponsorships as a direct result of managing negotiation processes with local companies
- Contributing directly to the school moving from 35% 5 A*-Cs to 50% whilst in charge of teaching and learning
- Winning the Granada Award for Schools Working in the Community in recognition for community work undertaken at the College

1996-2000   **Head of Humanities & ICT Coordinator**
- Responsible for the management of the humanities faculty whilst coordinating the delivery of ICT across the curriculum

Key Achievements
- Leading the strategic development of ICT and overseeing major developments and purchases
- Managing the introduction of one of the first school remote access facilities in the country as well as coordinating DCSF funded video conferencing projects
- Developing new courses within Humanities with considerable success enjoyed in examination results

CAREER SUMMARY cont.

1989-1996   **WATERGATE COMMUNITY COLLEGE, WATERGATE**
                  Head of Humanities & Professional Mentor

- Managing the Initial Teacher Training & Professional Development and initiating the mentoring programme for trainee teachers

Key Achievements
- Writing and implementing a new appraisal policy to facilitate substantial improvements in performance management
- Making a significant personal contribution to curriculum development using cross-curricular themes
- Leading the College's environmental work resulting in it winning the Radio Solent's Environmental Challenge in 1996

1980-1989   **THE QUEEN'S SCHOOL, NEWTOWN**
                  Lower School Humanities coordinator

- Successfully coordinating disparate members of staff from different departments to deliver an integrated humanities course covering history, geography and RE

Key Achievements
- Spearheading the development of resources including the use of visual-audio and information technology

EDUCATION AND QUALIFICATIONS

NPQH: National Professional Qualification for Headship
PGCE: Geography
BA (Hons): Geography – 2:1
3 A Levels: English, French and Geography
8 O Levels: Including English and Mathematics

PROFESSIONAL DEVELOPMENT

[Ofsted and Inspection Framework (Key Note Speaker)
[RAISEonline
[SSAT's Data Enabler Toolkit
[Certificate in Further Professional Studies

PUBLICATIONS

[Globalising the Curriculum (published in Teaching History, AG Publications, September 2008)

FURTHER SKILLS

I.T. Proficiency: Word, Excel, Access, Fireworks, Publisher, Photoshop, Internet and Email
Languages: Intermediate French

INTERESTS AND ACTIVITIES

Currently include: Hill Walking, Football, Cricket, Rugby Union and Reading (Classics & History)

REFERENCES ARE AVAILABLE ON REQUEST

Page 2 of 2

Gareth Hobson

1 Any Road, Anytown AN1 1CV
Telephone: 07700 900 235
Email: garethhobson@example.com

PROFESSIONAL PROFILE

A dedicated and dynamic professional combining strong business acumen with extensive experience in managing internal and external audit processes. Attentive to detail with a logical and analytical approach to solving complex problems and issues. Able to demonstrate an excellent knowledge of Sarbanes-Oxley, UK and US GAAP regulations with the proven ability to ensure full compliance therewith whilst also being proficient in internal audit and business processes. Possesses excellent interpersonal, communication and negotiation skills, the ability to influence business critical decisions and to formulate positive internal and external relationships. Works effectively on own initiative with the organisation and time management required to complete assignments on time and to the required quality standard. Enjoys being part of, as well as leading, a successful and productive audit team and thrives in highly pressurised and challenging working environments.

CAREER SUMMARY

2001–date   **Accent on Accounting**
    Manager – Internal Audit Services

- Commencing employment as an Associate on a graduate training scheme working in external audit before gaining promotion through Senior Associate to Manager in internal audit
- Responsible for a number of key clients including Bunny Bros

Responsibilities and Achievements (Bunny Bros)
- Managing internal business process and licensee audit reviews for Bunny Home Video Entertainment as part of a global co-source contract across Asia Pacific, Europe and Middle East
- Completing Sarbanes-Oxley reviews in the UK, France, Germany, Japan and Canada to facilitate full regulatory compliance
- Performance managing up to four UK and overseas based team members including setting objectives, providing coaching and work programmes, and contributing to their continuing professional development
- Ensuring accuracy and attention to detail when drafting internal audit reports, comprising information on issues, risks and innovative control recommendations
- Personally responsible for identifying claims in favour of Bunny Bros totalling $ 1.1 million against all five licensees' audits withtwo instances enabling the recovery of the audit fee
- Designing and implementing a strategy for long-term IT development within the business to enable the establishment of an e-commerce offering
- Producing budgets and long-term forecasts for subsequent presentation to the Banks
- Successfully increasing product lines by 300% whilst also reducing overall stockholding value by 25%
- Additionally driving down staff fixed costs by 20%

Responsibilities and Achievements (other clients)
- Managing internal audit plans for Computerserve plc, Neston plc and Express Train Group across EMEA and Asia Pacific involving extensive reporting to Partner and Directors and each respective Head of Internal Audit with excellent feedback received from each client

CAREER SUMMARY cont.

- Negotiating and securing a £25 million group distribution contract resulting in a 10% reduction in overall distribution costs
- Driving down packaging costs by 28% as a result of initiating a reverse auctioning programme
- Creating and implementing a stock disposal programme, linked to catalogue printing, resulting in savings of £800,000 over two years
- Playing a lead role in the seamless completion of a £1.7 million office development and relocation project
- Redesigning the distributor commission package resulting in £500,000 savings per annum
- Introducing a new credit control system to enable a reduction in bad debts from 2.5% of turnover to just 0.8%
- Making a significant personal contribution to an overall growth in turnover from £20 million to £80 million in six years

General Achievements

- Initiating and concluding successful negotiations with Irish authorities to achieve a 50% reduction in output VAT
- Playing a pivotal role as Counselling Manager for five members of staff tasked with providing objective career guidance and assessing annual performance

EDUCATION AND QUALIFICATIONS

ACA: Institute of Chartered Accountants of Scotland (2004)
BSc (Hons): Business Economics – 2:1 (2001)
4 A Levels: Economics, French, German and General Studies (1998)
11 GCSEs: Including Business Studies, English and Mathematics (1996)

PROFESSIONAL DEVELOPMENT

- The Accent on Accounting Business Diploma (ongoing)
- Sarbanes-Oxley Training and Expertise
- Six Sigma Orientation and Methodology Training

PROFESSIONAL MEMBERSHIPS

Associate Member: Institute of Cost & Executive Accountants (ICEA)

FURTHER SKILLS

IT Proficiency: Word, Excel, PowerPoint, MyClient, Aura, TeamMate and SAP
Languages: Intermediate French, German and Hindi; Basic Italian

INTERESTS AND ACTIVITIES

Currently include: Tennis, Snooker and Film/Cinema (especially Hitchcock)

REFERENCES ARE AVAILABLE ON REQUEST

ADMINISTRATION

SUSAN FARRER

1 Any Road, Anytown AN1 1CV
Telephone: 01632 960 551
Mobile: 07700 900 481
Fax: 01632 960 656
Email: susanfarrer@example.com

PROFESSIONAL PROFILE

A resourceful, hard-working and dedicated individual with outstanding administrative and organisational skills and the proven ability to develop and implement effective new systems and procedures. Possesses excellent IT skills with advanced knowledge of MS Office, is quick to grasp new ideas and concepts and always keen to develop new skills and expertise. Able to work well both independently and as part of a productive team, demonstrating the motivation and multi-tasking abilities required to meet demanding deadlines whilst maintaining the highest of standards. Articulate and proactive, combines a professional and confident approach with excellent interpersonal skills and can communicate concisely at all levels.

CAREER SUMMARY

2006–date   Business Improvement Project Coordinator, Luton Ltd, London

- Working as PA to the Programme Director with responsibility for developing, implementing and monitoring efficient office activities in addition to managing all correspondence
- Undertaking diary and event management and making travel arrangements as well as organising meetings with associated catering and accommodation
- Providing effective secretarial support and managing holiday requests and absence due to sickness for the project team and overseeing the office facilities
- Responsible as Project Coordinator for delivering a number of systems enhancements within the business improvement programme
- Consulting with staff at all levels to identify policy and best practice requirements as well as managing the Policy & Best Practice intranet site
- Making key contributions to the management of the communication plan whilst monitoring and updating programme plans on a wider basis
- Liaising with individual project teams to ensure the delivery of objectives whilst tracking the overall project progress and deliverables
- Preparing comprehensive consolidated project status and performance reports for the OpEx team

2005–2006   PA/Office Manager, Leonardo plc, Godalming

- Undertaking PA duties including diary management for the IT Director in addition to managing team expenses, diaries and schedules and the IT budget
- Coordinating travel and accommodation arrangements as well as managing meeting schedules and organising lunches and refreshments
- Creating a range of documentation including presentations, correspondence, memos and reports as well as taking minutes when required, and providing secretarial support for the team and management
- Carrying out IT procurement activities, monitoring third-party suppliers to ensure consistently good value as well as maintaining the IT standard catalogue
- Overseeing the smooth operation of the procurement process, managing work queues and evaluating performance tracking activities
- Compiling reports highlighting costs of products and services as well as preparing data for forecasting and budgeting
- Undertaking office management activities with responsibility for stationery, equipment and company mobile phones as well as organising company and rental vehicles
- Keeping accurate records of holiday and absence in addition to establishing data tracking systems and developing efficient office procedures

Page 1 of 2

CAREER SUMMARY cont.

2003–2005   Sales and Training Coordinator, Simon Says Leisure, Woking

- Working in a sales analyst role, preparing daily and monthly spreadsheets on behalf of the sales team and creating sales and performance graphs, sales and marketing presentations
- Maintaining the sales database as well as producing business reports on sales and income from membership joining fees and reconciling monthly commissions and quarterly bonuses
- Coordinating training activities, managing an online training diary and organising training events as well as preparing training packs and issuing joining instructions
- Delivering administrative support in sales and marketing as well as collating the training report on a monthly basis and organising accommodation, travel and refreshments as required

2000–2003   Business Support Executive, Graphic Office Supplies, Guildford

- Developing and delivering the online ordering system and training internal staff in its use in addition to providing administration of online accounts and the back-office system
- Demonstrating the online system to customers before closing sales, following up with system training as required
- Compiling online tutorials and training packs as well as providing full helpdesk support for the system

1998–2000   PA/Marketing Coordinator, Anarchy Ltd, Winchester

- Providing comprehensive PA support for the Sales and Marketing Director in addition to managing sales budgets and expenses and undertaking secretarial duties for the sales and marketing team
- Coordinating exhibitions, conferences and seminars in addition to organising mail shots and sourcing promotional items, liaising effectively with a range of suppliers and agencies
- Producing sales and marketing presentations as well as maintaining the database and delivering training as required

EDUCATION AND QUALIFICATIONS

ECDL	European Computer Driving Licence
NVQ2	Customer Services
5 GCSEs	Including English and Mathematics

FURTHER SKILLS

IT proficiency	MS Office, MS Project and SPSS
Languages	Intermediate Spanish

OTHER DETAILS

Driving licence	Full/Clean
Interests include	Hockey (captained Luton 2nd Eleven), Yoga and Violin

REFERENCES ARE AVAILABLE ON REQUEST

JAMES ROWE

1 Any Road, Anytown AN1 1CV
Telephone: 01632 960 791 (Home); 07700 900 214 (Mobile)
Email: jamesrowe@example.com

PROFESSIONAL PROFILE

An extremely conscientious, authoritative and dedicated individual, who enjoys the demands of high levels of accuracy and concentration, and flourishes with increased responsibilities. Quick and keen to learn, is diligent and meticulous, thrives in a demanding environment and relishes a technical challenge. Naturally self-motivated with lots of energy and enthusiasm, works well on own initiative and performs effectively under pressure. Personable and assured, possesses excellent interpersonal skills, can communicate concisely at all levels, and is a strong team builder and a natural leader, able to encourage disparate personalities to work in a team structure.

OBJECTIVE

Now looking for a new and challenging position, one that will make best use of current skills and experience and enable further personal and professional development towards the role of Production Supervisor.

CAREER SUMMARY

1995–date *Production Section Leader, John Velux Home Appliances, London*

- Initially starting as a programmer and setter of Bridgeport CNC machines, using both Fanuc and Heidenhain controls
- Gaining promotion to Production Section Leader of Aluminium Production
- Undertaking full accountability to meet the production schedule
- Successfully supervising and motivating 15 members of staff, delegating jobs and prioritising a production plan to achieve production targets and maintain all quality standards to ISO 9000
- Training all staff to high standards, encouraging precise tooling manufacture and facilitating the production of quality components
- Ordering tooling and assisting in the design and manufacture of production jigs and fixtures
- Implementing production efficiency and ensuring all personnel work to extremely high standards of health and safety
- Undertaking responsibilities of Qualified First Aider, Fire Marshall, Health and Safety Representative and Pensions committee member

Key Achievements:

- 1998: completed a quality report, focusing on scrap and rejected parts
- Implemented changes reducing scrap reducing by 17%
- 1999: reduced CNC production cost by incorporating ancillary forming and de-burring operations into machine cycle time with an annual saving of £11,500
- 2002: reduced production costs through tooling modification, by reducing the amount of operations when fabricating cooker door trims and saving an annual £8,300
- 2007: reduced costs of sub-contractor anodising by using an alternative method of finishing and lacquering components
- Detailed to go to Germany to purchase an appropriate machine and complete trials, bought a £40,000 machine which repaid its cost within 12 months
- Achieved 13 years of 100% attendance at work

CAREER SUMMARY cont.

1976–1995   *Machinist Setter-Operator, Lockheed Precision Aviation (APPH), Slough*

- Undertaking a 4-year indentured apprenticeship in Mechanical Engineering with the company, working on lathes, milling, grinding machines and aircraft undercarriage assembly
- Gaining promotion to setter operator on conventional vertical and horizontal milling machines and lathes
- Gaining further promotion as setter operator on CNC milling machines (Mycenter, Toyoda, Milwaukee and Ajax) and CNC lathes (Okuma, Dean Smith and Grace)
- Achieving all production targets and ensuring the dimensional accuracy of components
- Completing all quality procedures to ISO 9000 standards

Key Achievements:
- Achieved City and Guilds qualifications in Engineering 1,2,3,4
- Edited programmes and modified tooling to improve production efficiency

EDUCATION AND QUALIFICATIONS

City & Guilds:	AutoCAD Mechanical Design, Pass (2001)
NVQ:	Engineering CNC Machining, Pass (1996)
City & Guilds:	Mechanical Engineering, Credit (1980)
6 O Levels:	Including English & Mathematics (1976)

FURTHER SKILLS

I.T. Proficiency:	Word, Excel, Lotus Notes, Internet and Email
Languages:	Basic French, German and Italian

PERSONAL DETAILS

Nationality:	British
Driving Licence:	Full/Clean
Health:	Excellent; non-smoker
Other Details:	Qualified First Aider and Fire Marshall

INTERESTS AND ACTIVITIES

Currently include: Swimming, Tennis, Soccer, Cycling, Theatre, Art Galleries and Museums

REFERENCES ARE AVAILABLE ON REQUEST

GEORGE BUCHANAN

1 Any Road, Anytown AN1 1CV
Telephone: 01632 960 575 (Home); 07700 900 183 (Mobile)
Email: georgebuchanan@example.com

PROFESSIONAL PROFILE

An experienced and highly motivated business professional, with a proven record of success in both the travel and property industries, with a wealth of transferable skills, including outstanding interpersonal and staff management abilities. A capable organiser, quick to grasp – and make good use of – new ideas and information, and reliable and conscientious in all he takes on. Enjoys leading, motivating and being part of a productive team; equally comfortable working on own initiative. Possesses exemplary planning skills and accustomed to operating under considerable pressure, remaining calm and effective and prioritising wisely.

OBJECTIVE

Now looking for a challenging new position, one which will make good use of existing skills and experience whilst enabling further personal and professional development – ideally within account or event management, and connected to food or the hospitality industry.

CAREER SUMMARY

2006–present　　*Owner/Director, Munch, Haywards Heath*

- Starting up and developing a highly successful business supplying fruit and vegetables to various public sector institutions
- Researching and preparing tenders; winning valuable contracts – for instance, with Leeds and Nottingham City Councils
- Dealing with all aspects of client relations and sales management, together with detailed financial control and reporting
- Managing two full-time staff and directing and monitoring the contracted-out packaging and delivery service

Key achievements
- Swiftly building turnover over three years from zero to an annual contract value of £1.5 million
- Winning – against considerable competition – a 12-month extension of the substantial Leeds contract

2002–2006　　*Business Liaison Manager, Rural Enterprises, Slough*

- Assisting with post-Foot & Mouth rural business development – visiting a wide variety of enterprises and drawing on business experience to advise on marketing and management
- Initiating, planning and managing a number of well-attended locally-orientated promotional events and exhibitions

Key achievement
- Organising and overseeing all aspects of a lively three-day food festival, with 10,000 visitors

CAREER SUMMARY cont.

1998–2002   *General Manager/Director, The Scaynes Hill Hotel, Coniston Cold*

- Playing a key role in the building plans, fitting out and launch of a brand-new, 40-bedroom hotel on the edge of the Yorkshire Dales
- Responsible for recruiting and training the front-of-house team, establishing high standards of customer service and leading by example
- Dealing very capably with the crucial areas of PR, sales and marketing, and subsequently delivering 60% occupancy within 12 months of opening

Key achievement

- Winning Yorkshire Tourist Board and National CATEY 'Best Newcomer' awards

1990–1998   *Area Sales Manager, Register International Hotels*

- Heading a team of four Divisional Sales Managers and responsible for meeting the regional and national sales targets for a predominantly four-star hotel group
- Managing and successfully retaining the group's key accounts, with clients from government, banking and various agencies

EDUCATION AND QUALIFICATIONS

6 O Levels: Including English and Mathematics, all A–C (1983)

FURTHER SKILLS

IT Proficiency: MS Word, Excel, PowerPoint, Publisher and Access

PERSONAL DETAILS

Driving Licence: Full/Clean
Health: Excellent; non-smoker

INTERESTS AND ACTIVITIES

Currently include: Riding, going to the gym and football and creative writing

REFERENCES ARE AVAILABLE ON REQUEST

EXECUTIVE

Christopher Cooper

address: **1 Any Road, Anytown AN1 1CV**
telephone: **01632 960 939**
mobile: **07700 900 232**
email: **christophercooper@example.com**

Professional profile

A dynamic senior manager with extensive procurement operations and project management experience within the retail sector. A competent strategist capable of developing innovative plans and activities designed to facilitate competitive growth and competitive superiority. Possesses excellent interpersonal, communication and negotiation skills, the ability to influence decisions and to develop positive relationships both internally and externally. Enjoys being part of, as well as managing, motivating, training and developing, a successful and productive team and thrives in highly pressurised and challenging working environments.

Career summary

2004–date   **J SAINSBURY PLC**

2008–date   **Senior Project Manager – International Buying Office**
- Creating and implementing an innovative strategy to facilitate the seamless integration of Turkey and Asia into IBO procurement
- Additionally responsible for the development of a key strategy for the Global Direct Sourcing function

2008   **Senior Buying Manager – Added Value Foods**
- Fully accountable for the Beers, Ales and Cider category with £711 million sales delivered across the UK and ROI on brands and own brand products
- Providing management and support to a dedicated buying and marketing team and motivating them towards the achievement of objectives
- Successfully streamlining processes whilst creating a buying scale by leveraging the international business
- Proactively managing increasing challenges including rising costs of commodities, duty and energy to enable J Sainsbury to outperform the market and retain market share

Key Achievements
- Successfully overachieving budgeted sales by 12% (£25 million) whilst negotiating an additional £12 million in business plan support

2004–2008   **Head of Category – Produce Group Sourcing**
- Personally responsible for the creation and implementation of a Produce Central Buying Process to leverage economy of scale for J Sainsbury Group and facilitate subsequent cost savings
- Managing day to day operations within Group Sourced Fresh Produce Category (vegetables, salads and horticulture) with responsibility for strategic growth and development
- Responsible for €208 million sales across the Group with a team of Buyers and Buying Managers based in UK, Ireland, Slovakia, Czech Republic, Hungary and Poland
- Delivering increased product quality and reduced costs in accordance with customer expectations as a direct result of developing capability within the team and the supply base

Key Achievements
- Receiving an award from Sainsbury's Main Board for delivering group savings of £20 million in the first year whilst simultaneously overachieving the savings budget by £800,000
- Consolidating and establishing fresh hubs in Czech Republic, Slovakia, Poland and Hungary to leverage economy of scale
- Leading on the implementation of a new buying structure, involving substantial operational change, new processes and systems to enable a move towards a Group Procurement Strategy and the implementation of best practices
- Playing a pivotal role as a senior member of a leadership team tasked with creating and expanding a multi-national produce buying team in the UK with achievements including delivering 60% of produce and horticulture procurement in CE and 5.5% of produce procurement in UK
- Introducing an innovative new range of cut flowers in CE with an annual budget of €20 million delivering 25% margin
- Establishing direct procurement from growers on Indian and Thai cut flowers to facilitate the delivery of the direct sourcing strategy

Page 1 of 2

Career summary cont.

2003–2004   **UNITED WORLD COMMUNICATIONS, NAIROBI, KENYA**
Owner / Executive Director
- Establishing and managing a communications centre in Nairobi to provide unique communications options for the general and expatriate business community to enable NGOs and Missions to securely transact the financial aspects of their organisations

1997–2003   **TESCO UK LTD**
Head of Fresh Produce Procurement UK & ROI
- Commencing employment in a retail management and store expansion capacity before progressing through to Head of Produce responsible for seasonal non-food buying for UK and ROI
- Managing departmental operations covering 400 stores and 7 regional distribution centres with full accountability for 13% of company sales, £90 million annual turnover and profit margins in excess of 40%

Key Achievements
- Successfully doubling sales participation from 6.5% to 13% whilst driving a strong annual like for like of 15% and overall growth of 35% over 3 years
- Establishing a successful 7 days fresh cut flower business delivering 500% growth in the first year

1995–1996   **REGAL MOVING & STORAGE INC, NEW YORK, USA**
Director

1992–1994   **REPAKS TRANSPORTE GESMBHH, VIENNA, AUSTRIA**
Managing Director / Owner

1990–1992   **UN DISENGAGEMENT OBSERVER FORCES, DAMASCUS, SYRIA**
Military Police

Formal qualifications

Leadership Development Programme (2009)
- Business Leaders of Today
- Create the Vision & the Need for Change
- Sell & Communicate with Impact
- Gain Commitment & Engage Team
- Business Plan

Professional training

- Negotiation Skills
- Ethical Buying
- Advanced Negotiation Skills
- Situational Leadership

- Range Management
- Competition Act
- Coaching & Feedback
- Performance Management

Other details

Languages   Fluent German
IT proficiency   Word, Excel, PowerPoint and GMIS
Driving licence   Full/Clean
Interests include Swimming, Cycling, Triathlons and Art (Painting)

References are available on request

NATALIE SHAH

1 Any Road, Anytown AN1 1CV
Telephone: 01632 960 941; Mobile: 07700 900 935; Fax: 01632 960 316
Email: natalieshah@example.com

PROFESSIONAL PROFILE

➢ *A versatile and results-oriented professional who specialises in sourcing and buying products from UK and overseas markets requiring strong supplier relationships*

➢ *Familiar with all aspects of the consumer electronics market with particular emphasis on buying, marketing and e-commerce*

➢ *Possesses excellent interpersonal skills and the ability to communicate and negotiate concisely and articulately at all levels*

➢ *Attentive to detail with a practical approach to problem solving and the organisation required to ensure that deadlines, budgets and objectives are achieved*

➢ *Enjoys being part of a successful and productive team and thrives in highly pressurised and challenging working environments*

OBJECTIVE

Currently looking for a new and challenging position within the corporate sector, one which will make best use of existing skills and experience acquired in privately owned companies whilst enabling further personal and professional development.

CAREER SUMMARY

2005–date   FAR EAST MANAGER, *ABC Group LTD*

- Headhunted by the Chairman of this small family company specialising in the wholesale of consumer electronics products in the UK
- Tasked with the sole running and development of the company's interest in the China market, importing health food supplements, with full P&L and stockholding accountability
- Successfully increasing gross profits by 100% in the first full year with the business
- Driving sales into the UK health food market and achieving new sales of more than £1 million with projections for the following year of £3 million
- Cold calling prospective new customers and establishing a credit rating for them as well as sourcing products and negotiating prices with China
- Liaising extensively with UK customers to agree product specifications, sale prices and lead times
- Responsible for ensuring the accurate completion of associated paperwork including import documentation, which required liaising with Freight Forwarders and Port Health, with full accountability for the safe delivery of customer orders
- Travelling extensively to China to meet with new suppliers and to assess potential new products
- Actively involved in planning and organising the company's participation in a Health Food national event in September 2007

CAREER SUMMARY cont.

1985–2005   MANAGING DIRECTOR, *Sound & Vision Ltd*

- Commencing employment in the retail outlet before gaining a series of promotions culminating in the role of Managing Director for this privately owned company
- Negotiating terms and setting prices of consumer electronic and white goods product categories whilst maintaining awareness of budgetary constraints
- Playing a pivotal role in the launch and implementation of an e-commerce site, www.unbeatable.co.uk
- Interviewing, recruiting, training and mentoring new buyers into the business
- Setting budgets and forecasting sales whilst maintaining full P&L accountability
- Analysing buying trends and utilising this for the purposes of determining stock holding
- Creating and executing highly successful buying and sales promotions
- Responsible for a stock holding valued at up to £5 million and playing a key role in both in-store and online promotional activities
- Utilising strong skills in communication and negotiation to build mutually beneficial relationships with suppliers
- Establishing and developing concessions within the London stores Harrods and Selfridges

1982–1985   CLERK/CASHIER, *National Westminster Bank*

EDUCATION AND QUALIFICATIONS

9 O Levels   Including English and Mathematics

FURTHER SKILLS

IT Proficiency   Word, Excel, PowerPoint, Internet and Email
Languages   Basic French

PERSONAL DETAILS

Driving Licence   Full/Clean
Health   Excellent; non-smoker

INTERESTS AND ACTIVITIES

Include   Running, Keeping Fit and Cooking

REFERENCES ARE AVAILABLE ON REQUEST

RACHEL GRIFFITHS

1 Any Road, Anytown AN1 1CV
Telephone: 01632 960 898 (Home); 07700 900 623 (Mobile)
Email: rachelgriffiths@example.com

PROFESSIONAL PROFILE

A positive and professional retail and service manager who is passionate about delivering exceptional customer service standards whilst ensuring the achievement of demanding targets and corporate objectives. With a proven track record of achieving success in merchandising, driving sales, promoting brands and increasing turnover. A motivational and inspirational manager capable of coaching and empowering individuals to fulfil their potential as well as make a significant contribution to the business. Consistently demonstrates insight and shrewd judgement with the ability to devise innovative solutions to problems.

EDUCATION AND QUALIFICATIONS

CPC: Unit 1: Financial Management, Health & Safety Contract Law, Wakefield College (2012)
Examinations for Units 2 and 3 scheduled for 2013 will result in full Certificate of Professional Competence

CLAIT: OCR Level, Selby College (1999)

CAREER SUMMARY

1998–date   *Group Manager, Adams Company Shops, Castleford*

- Responsible for managing two Adams staff shops serving staff, retired staff and contractors based at Castleford and at Halifax with full responsibility for all aspects of store management including staffing, premises, stock control, shrinkage, customer service and merchandising.
- Accountable for leading a team of one supervisor, 2 full-time staff and 4 part-time staff to achieve sales and drive brand awareness amongst new and existing clients
- Recruiting, supervising, leading and motivating staff by maintaining excellent communication channels, conducting appraisals and ensuring they have the skills and tools to do their individual jobs effectively
- Conducting 6 weekly meetings with clients to review the status of their accounts and develop future strategic and operational plans
- Motivating and leading staff to exceed team targets and KPIs covering sales, customer satisfaction, training and budget control
- Controlling stock levels with due regard for procurement, shrinkage and cashflow
- Monitoring training and development for staff, analysing training needs, making recommendations for solutions and maintaining records
- Conducting audits to ensure stores comply with all regulatory requirements including Health & Safety, COSHH, risk assessment and finance
- Accountable for all financial transactions within the group including banking and agreeing/paying salaries
- Developing and implementing improved procedures and processes to ensure better and more consistent service throughout the stores
- Promoted to Manager in 2005 and Group Manager in 2007 as a result of outstanding performance and appraisal reviews

Page 1 of 2

CAREER SUMMARY cont.

1994–1998   *Store Manager, J&I Store, Knottingley*

- Fully accountable for all aspects of running a convenience store including managing the premises, security and housekeeping as well as ensuring compliance with all regulatory and legal guidelines, procedures and requirements
- Recruiting, motivating and supervising full-time and part-time staff, planning rotas and providing training, coaching and support to ensure they fulfil their potential and contribute effectively to the business
- Successfully devising and implementing a Customer Service Enhancement Programme, ensuring the whole team provide outstanding levels of service at all times and dealing personally with any customer complaints or problems
- Creatively planning promotions and implementing programmes to maximise merchandising opportunities and thus increase sales
- Controlling all store budgets and providing management information about sales, margins, forecasts, expenditure and local promotional or product opportunities
- Selected through merit to carry out the duties of the Area Manager's role during maternity leave absence

1977–1994   *Receptionist, A B Jones, Castleford*

- Appointed as a check-out operator and rapidly promoted to Receptionist
- Responsible for greeting all visitors and taking all in-bound calls with professionalism and sincerity
- Providing administrative support to colleagues by organising meetings, dealing with post, managing the file archiving programme and carrying out ad-hoc tasks as required
- Acting as the first point of contact for customer complaints and returns, and dealing with them if possible or escalating to an appropriate colleague

---

IT PROFICIENCY

- Nexus, EPoS, Word, Excel and PowerPoint

PERSONAL DETAILS

Driving Licence: Full/Clean
Health: Excellent; non-smoker

INTERESTS AND ACTIVITIES

Currently include: DIY, cooking, reading and hiking

REFERENCES ARE AVAILABLE ON REQUEST

PATRICIA HEPWORTH

1 Any Road, Anytown AN1 1CV
Telephone: 01632 960 739 (Home); 07700 900 709 (Mobile)
Email: patriciahepworth@example.com

Professional Profile

A dedicated and results-driven senior manager with a highly successful background in the achievement of profitable business growth through the creation and execution of successful sales and marketing strategies. Experienced in working with leading brands in the competitive retail and automotive industries with the primary focus on exceeding expectations for customer service delivery whilst ensuring optimum brand impact. Possesses excellent interpersonal, communication and negotiation skills and the ability to develop and maintain mutually beneficial internal and external relationships. Enjoys being part of, as well as managing, motivating and training, a successful and productive team, and thrives in highly pressurised and challenging working environments.

Career Summary

2005–2009   TYRES UK LTD
Freelance Consultant/Interim Network Development Manager

- Project managing the redevelopment of the retail sales strategy across the UK market with the ultimate aim of facilitating business performance improvements
- Successfully developing multi-channel solutions including instigating a new HiQ Fast Fit Franchise proposition
- Playing a pivotal role in the design and development of a class-leading B2C eBusiness website
- Working in close conjunction with external professionals to create and implement a retail network representation plan
- Actively involved in developing a new retail store concept and in redrafting all contractual agreements and process/procedure manuals
- Coordinating the pitch and scoping process for the selection of a staff training and development academy

1999–2005   BDW GROUP
2005–2005   Managing Director, BDW Contact Ltd

- Fully accountable for the establishment and management of a new business arm specialising in the provision of telemarketing services requiring the development of an independent customer base
- Collaborating with professionals and third parties to set up the infrastructure for the company and coordinating the recruitment, selection and training of 15 members of staff
- Planning and organising a highly successful launch programme and driving the business forward to break-even three months ahead of projections
- Introducing a range of B2B and B2C services and facilitating the provision of 24-hour service by business partnership in conjunction with an external agency

2000–2004   Operations Director

- Providing management and support to up to 68 members of staff and motivating them towards the achievement of optimum service delivery standards to facilitate customer satisfaction and maximum revenue generation
- Maintaining full profit and loss accountability up to £5 million whilst achieving a year-on-year growth in revenue of more than 10%
- Initiating half yearly service reviews with major blue chip, retail clients and formalising account planning to ensure best practice resulting directly in recognition for excellence in customer surveys
- Developing and implementing new billing and forecasting systems which significantly improved overall efficiency
- Enabling a 5% increase in actual gross margin in 1 year through the implementation of a staff incentive scheme

Career Summary cont.

1999–2000   **Account Director**

- Working in close conjunction with key client representatives to develop marketing strategies and point-of-sale materials on behalf of retail partners
- Negotiating and securing £120,000 in bespoke systems development revenue and playing a key role in increasing monthly revenue from £12,000 to £100,000

1996–1999   **WORDS PICTURES SOUNDS**
                    Managing Director

- Setting up and developing a full service design agency from the initial business planning, financial forecasting and business strategy development through to building and retaining the customer base
- Successfully securing and effectively managing contracts with leading brands including Audi, One 2 One and Cadbury for the provision of a range of creative services including media creative, brochure design, corporate identity and hard point of sale
- Achieving approved supplied status with Audi and One 2 One and delivering sustained income growth with the turnover increasing from £75,000 in 1996 to £750,000 in 1999

1983–1996   **VAG (UK) LTD**
                    Audi A8 Project Manager

- Commencing employment as a Trainee Field Sales Manager on behalf of the sole importers of Volkswagen and Audi vehicles and parts into the UK
- Gaining a series of promotions through various product, marketing, operations and advertising management positions, both head office and field based
- Ultimately undertaking the head office role of Audi A8 Project Manager tasked with the development and promotion of the brand and the vehicle within the luxury market with a total spend of £1.5 million

Education and Qualifications

4 A Levels   Mathematics, Economics, History and General Studies
8 O Levels   Including English and Mathematics

Professional Development

- Management Development Programme
- Marketing Management
- Presentation Skills
- Finance for Non-financial Managers

- Effective Man Management
- Appraisal Training
- Team Building
- Creativity Training

IT Skills

- Word, Excel, Access, PowerPoint, Internet and Email

Personal Details

Driving Licence   Full/Clean
Health   Excellent; non-smoker
Interests   Squash, Golf, Reading (current affairs), Theatre and Cuisine

References Are Available On Request

Page 2 of 2

Tony Crockford

1 Any Road, Anytown AN1 1CV
Telephone: 07700 900 218
Email: tonycrockford@example.com

PROFESSIONAL PROFILE

A dynamic and results-driven professional with a highly successful background in sales, account management and new business development. Committed to achieving and exceeding demanding targets and business objectives whilst remaining focused on providing an exceptional standard of service to international and UK clients. Possesses excellent interpersonal, communication and negotiation skills, the ability to influence decisions and to develop positive internal and external relationships. Enjoys being part of, as well as managing and motivating, a successful and productive team and thrives in highly pressurised and challenging working environments.

CAREER SUMMARY

2008–date   VAUCAN-HAMSTER LTD, Sales Associate

- Playing a key role as a Sales Associate within the newly established Marketing Business Development Department set up as a business development project to assist in generating opportunities across four practice verticals: general enterprise, industrial, technical and consumer products
- Personally responsible for driving revenue growth across these verticals by collaborating with clients on the provision of consulting and training services according to their needs utilising a range of problem solving, project execution and business process improvement applications
- Actively involved in outbound calling to facilitate the identification and qualification of sales leads across all practices
- Planning and executing innovative campaigns, including direct mail, webcasts, catalogue distribution and thought leadership, to generate new sales leads in EMEA and NA regions
- Developing positive relationships with potential clients, establishing their business needs and developing solutions based around Vaucan-Hamster services
- Preparing and delivering successful pitches to director, senior and middle management level prospects
- Additionally responsible for preparing and presenting detailed campaign analysis and reports to practice leaders

Key Achievements

- Playing a key role in promoting cross practice value propositions for consulting engagements and executive training solutions to develop strategic and operational problem solving and decision making, project management and business process improvements for issue resolution
- Contributing directly to the new department delivering 98% of leads target/plan and 98% of revenue target/plan within the first year
- Personally responsible for bringing in new leads to the organisation with values ranging from £10,000 to £50,000
- Currently involved in developing partnership deals within strategically aligned markets and territories within the Middle East
- Utilising previous expertise in developing internal departmental processes to lead on the creation and re-design of departmental systems to standardise project execution and campaign management/analysis

2005–2008   MEGA MEDIA LTD, Sales Executive (temporary)

- Initially undertaking a telesales based role for the regional lifestyle publication tasked with selling all forms of advertising space from classified to display page
- Gaining rapid promotion, after just 2 months, to a field based role covering two SE territories/publications with full accountability for the complete sales cycle including presenting at field appointments and closing agreements
- Liaising directly with events editors and photographers to facilitate appropriate coverage of planned events

Key Achievements

- Achieving personal recognition as the top sales person in the company despite only being employed on a 6-month contract
- Facilitating a sales growth for the area by 27% and £184k during the first year

2002–2005   AMOUR DISTRIBUTION LTD, Head of International Sales

- Responsible for the account management of key sub-distribution partnerships involving regular sales and strategy meetings at director level and overseas business meetings and visits
- Providing comprehensive advice to clients on all aspects of retail marketing, press and radio promotions
- Generating sales and budget analysis reports to enable the communication of departmental sales progress and performance

Page 1 of 2

CAREER SUMMARY cont.

Key Achievements
- Enjoying considerable success in terms of delivering in excess of £3.5 million annual department budgets
- Achieving year-on-year sales increases having successfully forecasted and planned departmental budgets
- Piloting and managing the successful development of a CD sub-distribution network in key overseas territories including USA, Canada, Australia, Germany, Benelux, Spain and France and concluding negotiations to secure exclusive product agreements
- Playing a pivotal role in the development of new business within existing networks of Direct Europe and UK export accounts having brokered exclusive product deals and campaigns
- Winning the International Trade & Export Award 2005 from Watford & North West London Business Association

2000–2002   RENAISSANCE DISTRIBUTION LTD, Import Singles Manager
- Responsible for the management of the singles department within the busy music wholesale company
- Managing an extensive portfolio of UK retail accounts with key clients such as HMV, Virgin and Tower, including delivering presentations to buyers and providing a first point of contact for all singles based product enquiries
- Attending weekly field sales meetings with London based major chain accounts and working with them to discuss and resolve any issues that may arise
- Recruiting and managing the dedicated telesales team and providing them with comprehensive training and support as required

Key Achievements
- Consistently achieving monthly and annual sales targets and playing a key role in delivering 20% business growth
- Contributing directly to the company achieving preferred supplier status with key national accounts for the import of singles products

1997–2000   VIRGIN LTD, Product Buyer
- Fully accountable for purchasing all chart and non-chart eligible singles products whilst maintaining awareness of budgetary constraints, sales and stock targets
- Developing and maintaining mutually beneficial relationships across an extensive network of UK suppliers

EDUCATION AND QUALIFICATIONS

DipHE:	Popular Music Performance
Drumtech Diploma:	Drums and Percussion
8 GCSEs:	Including English and Mathematics

PROFESSIONAL TRAINING

- Project Management: PMI Accredited
- Lean Manufacturing/Lean Office
- Incident Mapping
- Problem Solving & Decision Making for Investigations

KEY IT SKILLS

- Word, Excel, PowerPoint, Salesforce, Internet and Email

PERSONAL DETAILS

Driving Licence:	Full/Clean
Health:	Excellent; non-smoker
Interests include:	Running, Swimming, Golf and Guitar playing

REFERENCES ARE AVAILABLE ON REQUEST

James Catterall

1 Any Road, Anytown AN1 1CV
Telephone: 07700 900 826
Email: jamescatterall@example.com

PROFESSIONAL PROFILE

A highly experienced professional who effectively combines strong technical, problem-solving and planning capabilities to successfully deliver projects on time and on budget. Possesses excellent interpersonal skills and the ability to communicate professionally with clients, architects, suppliers and sub-contractors alike. Enjoys being part of, as well as managing and motivating, a successful and productive team and thrives in highly pressurised and challenging working environments.

CAREER SUMMARY

2003–date   MOORSIDE CONSTRUCTION, NOTTINGHAM
                 Site Manager

- Playing a pivotal role in the lifecycle management of a wide range of projects, ranging in scale and value, from the initial concept through to completion
- Providing management and support to all site personnel and developing and maintaining productive relationships with clients, architects and sub-contractors
- Monitoring and controlling all work activities with the primary focus on ensuring compliance with health and safety regulations
- Sourcing and recruiting sub-contractors and purchasing materials whilst maintaining awareness of budgetary constraints
- Working collaboratively to ensure that all projects are completed on time and within programme targets
- Producing and reviewing weekly and monthly progress reports and taking appropriate action to resolve any issues that are identified

Summary of Projects

- New build project of two luxury houses in Gerrard's Cross, Buckinghamshire (resale value £4 million)
- Refurbishment of 36 apartments in Nottingham City Centre (resale value £4.1 million)
- Modernisation of premises to accommodate glass company, Bridgwater (project costs £40,000)
- Preparing of sites for a construction phase including the demolition of existing buildings, Bridgwater
- High specification fit out of office units in Nottingham City Centre (project value for refurbishment £70,000)
- Development of several 4/5 bedroom luxury detached houses in Derbyshire (project value £900,000)
- Refurbishment of 4-bedroom bungalow in Derbyshire (refurbishment costs £30,000)
- Refurbishment of office premises in Surrey (costs £7,000)
- Fit out of 16 luxury apartments in Nottingham City Centre (resale value of £1.8 million)
- Development of 52 luxury retirement apartments in Plympton (resale value of £8.5 million)

2001–2003   TONY JARVIS, TEIGNMOUTH
                 Bricklayer / Chippies Mate

- Working both independently and alongside specific trades on a variety of new build and refurbishment projects with responsibility for the achievement of targets and compliance with health and safety legislation

2001   PRIVATE CLIENT, PLYMOUTH
                 General Builder

- Playing a key role in the modernisation and improvement of a 7-bedroom farm house in Oakhampton
- Undertaking a wide variety of tasks including installation of first-floor timbers, plastering, tiling and the formation of an extensive patio area

CAREER SUMMARY cont.

1999–2001   **PRIVATE CLIENT, FRANCE**
General Builder

- Working on the modernisation and improvement of various dwellings involving take-offs and materials ordering and planning the sequence of works

1997–1999   **BUDWEISER, GLASGOW**
Machine Operator / Maintenance Engineer

- Responsible for the safe operation of plant and machinery and for responding to any breakdowns that may arise

EDUCATION AND QUALIFICATIONS

NHBC NVQ: Construction Site Management Residential Development Level 4
NVQ: Mechanical & Electrical Engineering Level 2
Certificate: Agriculture
6 Standards: Including English and Mathematics

PROFESSIONAL TRAINING

- Construction Site Managers Safety Certificate
- Business/Construction Management Course
- Construction Certification Training
- First Aid at Work
- Fork Lift Certificate Class 1/2/3
- Manual Handling Certificate
- Abrasive Wheels Certificate
- Plastic Moulding Course

KEY IT SKILLS

- Word, Excel, Internet and Email

PERSONAL DETAILS

Driving Licence: Full/Clean
Health: Excellent; non-smoker
Other Details: Qualified First Aider

INTERESTS AND ACTIVITIES

Currently include: Gym Training, Paragliding, Off-road Motor Biking and Mountain Biking

REFERENCES ARE AVAILABLE ON REQUEST

RICKY WOOLF

1 Any Road, Anytown AN1 1CV
Telephone: 01632 960 898 (Home); 07700 900 138 (Mobile)
Email: rickywoolf@example.com

PROFESSIONAL PROFILE

A committed and proactive professional who specialises in the use of embedded design and programming techniques to develop creative and innovative robotic systems tailored towards specific project requirements. Quick to assimilate new ideas, concepts and cutting-edge technologies whilst demonstrating a logical and analytical approach to solving complex problems and issues. Able to work well on own initiative whilst demonstrating the organisation and prioritisation required to achieve tight deadlines and deliverables. A motivational and inspirational leader who enjoys being part of a successful and productive team, and thrives in highly pressurised and challenging working environments.

OBJECTIVE

Currently looking for a new and challenging position, one which will make best use of existing skills and experience whilst enabling further personal and professional development.

EDUCATION AND QUALIFICATIONS

MSc	Embedded Systems and Robotics – Distinction (2003)
	Thesis: *Compact Motion Tracking System for Human Rehabilitation*
BSc	Computer Science with Robotics & Intelligent Machines – 2.1 (2002)
	Thesis: *2D Mapping Mobile Robots in Unstructured Environments*
College Courses	Mathematics, Mechatronic Systems, Applied Dynamics and Electrical Control Theory

KEY TECHNICAL SKILLS

- Assembler, Embedded C, C++, Visual MFC, Linux, Java, OpenGL, Handle-C and VHDL

CAREER SUMMARY

2005–date   **Mobile Robotics Ltd, London**
              SENIOR RESEARCH ASSISTANT

- Playing a lead role in the research team tasked with developing a range of underwater robotic research vehicles, a £2.2 million project funded by the London Zoo
- Actively involved in the commercial aspects of the project to facilitate the achievement of demanding deadlines and deliverables, enabling the project to proceed to the next phase
- Providing a prompt and appropriate response to unforeseen mechanical and electrical design problems including making innovative decisions to prevent future repercussions
- Successfully developing a range of underwater robotic vehicles including both remote controlled and autonomous vehicles
- Additionally developing and testing materials, control and navigation systems to facilitate the achievement of operational functionality

CAREER SUMMARY cont.

2003–2005   **University of Exeter, Devon**
RESEARCH ASSISTANT

- Specifically responsible for the design and development of a low-cost, accurate, unobtrusive sensor to enable in-home, unaided rehabilitation on behalf of stroke victims
- Tasked with ensuring minimal hardware installation requirements within the patient's home environment requiring the team to overcome the obstacles associated with the use of camera tracking and body markers to enable the accurate mapping of limb movements
- Developing a wireless system using the Bluetooth protocol to minimise the problems usually associated with the weight of systems, the restriction of movement and visible wiring
- Overcoming the charging issues common with using very small batteries by designing a system that can be inductance charged at the end of each session

POSTGRADUATE TEACHING ASSISTANT

- Assisting with the delivery of laboratory sessions to undergraduates in the following subjects: Embedded Programming; C/C++ Programming; Electronic Hardware Design (PCB Design); Robotic Control Systems

1990–1998   **UVW Engineering Ltd, Cuckfield**
TECHNICAL ENGINEER

- Responsible for the repair and maintenance of agricultural vehicles including overhauling engines and transmission units and diagnosing and repairing faults

VOLUNTARY WORK

2005–date   **University of Cambridge/University of Oxford**
MACHINE CONSCIOUSNESS LABORATORY

- Actively involved in the resolution of design problems in the fields of electrical sensory feedback and mechanical systems within compliant anthropomimetic robotics

PERSONAL DETAILS

Driving Licence   Full/Clean
Health   Excellent; non-smoker

INTERESTS AND ACTIVITIES

Currently include   Fitness Training, Cooking and Astronomy
Other   Currently learning German

REFERENCES ARE AVAILABLE ON REQUEST

Phil Brown

1 Any Road, Anytown AN1 1CV
Telephone: 07700 900 002
Email: philbrown@example.com

PROFESSIONAL PROFILE

A dedicated and enthusiastic CCVP accredited professional who specialises in project managing innovative voice and data solutions to improve system stability, functionality and efficiency. Quick to familiarise himself with the latest technologies and industry developments whilst demonstrating a logical and analytical approach to solving complex problems and issues. Possesses excellent interpersonal and communication skills and the ability to develop and maintain positive internal and external relationships. Enjoys being part of, as well as leading, a successful and productive team and thrives in highly pressurised and challenging working environments.

CAREER SUMMARY

2001–date   BANK OF QUEBEC, Senior LAN/WAN & Voice Technical Analyst
- Working as part of the Trading Services Group tasked with providing 1st, 2nd and 3rd line support to 200 users and 100 traders in London and 40 traders in 8 European offices
- Generally responsible for the maintenance and programming of the Nortel/Cisco data network including programming routing, MLT, SMLT, Trunks, VLANs, VLAN tagging and ACLs
- Diagnosing and resolving faults with the BT ITS. Netrix dealerboard system, Nortel CS1000E VoIP and NiceLog call logging system
- Providing comprehensive support to end users of trading platforms including Bloomberg, Reuters, Orderboard and RDMS
- Additionally involved in providing Wintel support including AD, Server 2003, NAS, blade servers and blade workstations
- Developing and implementing procedures for new starters and leavers, and adding or deleting services in the bank

Key Projects and Achievements
- Playing a lead technical role in a major project to relocate to new offices including the implementation of new dealerboard/VoIP systems and a new Nortel/Cisco network
- Fully accountable for planning the move phases relating to the data and voice infrastructure for the new offices and working with external vendors to install and configure equipment
- Leading on the implementation of a new cabling/port database used to track all ports and connections in the infrastructure of the bank and producing procedures relating to moves/additions for audit purposes
- Taking appropriate action in response to audit results to facilitate improvements to the infrastructure network and voice systems and, as a result, achieving perfect scores from the audit team in 2004 and 2005
- Negotiating and securing a new maintenance contract for the voice/data systems resulting in substantial reductions in costs and a simultaneous improvement in SLA response times

2000–2001   NOKIA COMMUNICATIONS LTD, Senior Network Support Analyst
- Providing management and support to a team of eight 2nd and 3rd line support technicians tasked with the maintenance and fault diagnosis of the extensive Centrica voice network supporting 20,000 users and AXA network supporting 15,000 users
- Dialling into Mitel SX2000 and MD110 switches and collaborating with third-party suppliers to identify and rectify faults
- Meeting regularly with suppliers and liaising with third-party vendors with responsibility for escalating faults to SDMs and account managers for resolution
- Updating lines of business for priority faults and monitoring the team to ensure that issues are resolved in accordance with SLAs

Key Achievements
- Analysing procedures, escalation points and major faults and making subsequent recommendations to prevent the same problems from occurring

CAREER SUMMARY cont.

1998–2000   **EFG INFORMATION SYSTEMS, EFG Technician Level 6**

- Working within a busy dealing room environment with responsibility for the support, installation and fault finding of EFG MX and EFG TradeNet sites
- Supporting 150 traders including performing backups, amending records, adding/ceasing lines and implementing dealerboard changes

1997–1998   **EASTMAN INSURANCE SERVICES LTD, IT Communications Technician**

- Providing 2nd line support for six Meridian and two ISDX networked switches involving the use of Eclipse to log all calls received
- Responsible for the network infrastructure and for undertaking some project management for Meridian upgrades and moves
- Utilising Memotec clusters, case smartmuxes and kilostreams for the installation and maintenance of the RS232 and X25 data network

EDUCATION AND QUALIFICATIONS

CCNA: Cisco Certified Network Associate
CCVP: Cisco Certified Voice Professional
BTEC: National Diploma in I.T. Applications

PROFESSIONAL TRAINING

- VoIP
- Project Management
- BT ITS. Netrix
- HP Nas/Storage Mirroring
- Managing Windows Server 2003
- Implementing & Supporting XP
- Nortel Device Manager
- Nortel Networking
- Network+ N10-002

- MD 1000 Admin & Maintenance
- Telebusiness 200 Installation & Maintenance
- ISDN BRI/PRI Installation & Maintenance
- SX2000 Installation & Maintenance
- EFG MX
- Astro Data Communications/X25
- Wadsworth Cat 5 Installation
- BT Meridian Administrator

KEY TECHNICAL SKILLS

- Cisco IPT
- Nortel CS1000E IPT
- VoIP
- Nortel & Cisco LAN/WAN Networks
- BT ITS. Netrix Dealerboards
- EFG MX/TradeNet Dealerboards
- NiceLog
- Windows Server 2003
- Windows XP

- Mitel SX2000
- Mitel Telebusiness 2000
- Meridian PBX
- Meridian ACD
- CAT5 Cabling
- HP Openview
- TeVISTA
- Bloomberg
- Reuters D3000

PERSONAL DETAILS

Driving Licence: Full/Clean
Health: Excellent; non-smoker
Interests include: Fishing, Motor Sports and Football

REFERENCES ARE AVAILABLE ON REQUEST

Martin Wardle

address: 1 Any Road, Anytown AN1 1CV
telephone: 01632 960 326
mobile: 07700 900 285
e-mail: martinwardle@example.com

Professional profile

An enthusiastic and professional Web Designer, who enjoys being part of, as well as leading, a successful and productive team. Quick to grasp new ideas and concepts, and to develop innovative and creative solutions to problems. Able to work well on own initiative and can demonstrate the high levels of motivation required to meet the tightest of deadlines. Even under significant pressure, possesses a strong ability to perform effectively.

Objective

Now looking to build on extensive range of technical skills within a suitably challenging role. Keen to achieve further professional development.

Key technical skills

Adobe PhotoShop	Macromedia Dreamweaver	QuarkXPress
Adobe Illustrator	Macromedia Flash	Strata Studio Pro (3D)
Adobe Premiere	Macromedia Director	FTP Programs
Adobe After Effects	Poser	Bryce 3D
Adobe Acrobat	QTVR	Microsoft Excel
Microsoft PowerPoint	Equilibrium	Media Cleaner Pro

Career summary

2006–date   **Webmaster, Graphics UK, London**
- Working within a major print design company, tasked with developing their fledgling Web Department
- Assessing initial set-up requirements and implementing hardware and software solutions accordingly
- Training the team in the use of QuarkXPress, Beyond Press Pro, PhotoShop, Dreamweaver, Media Cleaner Pro, QTVR and Adobe Premiere
- Coordinating closely with Account Executives, actively soliciting new clients and nurturing existing client accounts, ensuring their needs and requirements were not only accommodated but surpassed
- Winning over many clients from larger companies, due to the extremely high standards of creative design work
- Training clients in subsequent website maintenance, particularly the use of Dreamweaver and its inbuilt FTP facility
- Initiating a company-wide changeover to a much faster ISP with enhanced technical support
- Clients include major blue chip companies such as the British Land Company and Millennium Diamonds as well as many high-profile government departments and agencies

Selected portfolio

www.website.com
www.onewithtext.com
www.onewithgraphics.com
www.personalwebsite.com

www.anotherwebsite.com
www.andanother.com
www.flashwebsite.com
www.onemoreexample.com

Education and qualifications

2003–2006   National Diploma in Graphic Design & Multimedia (First Class Honours)
Dublin Institute of Technology, Ireland

Key Modules: Web Design, Visual Communication, Multimedia, Print Design, Typography & Photography

Won the **Multimedia Student of the Year Award** and **Best Use of a Mac Award**

Professional development

- Team Leadership (Management Training Centre, 2009)
- Presentation Skills (Management Training Centre, 2008)

Personal details

Driving Licence   Full/Clean
Health   Excellent; non-smoker
Languages   Fluent French & German

Interests and activities

Currently include   Photography, Theatre & Amateur Dramatics, Football and Golf

References are available on request

Colin Smith

1 Any Road, Anytown AN1 1CV
Telephone: 01632 960 452 (Home); 07700 900 973 (Mobile)
Email: colinsmith@example.com

PROFESSIONAL PROFILE

A disciplined and dedicated professional with an expert knowledge of logistics, inventory and supply chain management acquired during more than 20 years service with the Royal Air Force. Specialises in delivering improvements in performance and efficiency through the implementation of Lean and value-adding processes whilst remaining focused on achieving service excellence. Able to work effectively on own initiative with the organisation and prioritisation required to achieve tight deadlines and budgets. Possesses excellent interpersonal, communication and negotiation skills, and the ability to develop positive relationships both internally and externally. Enjoys being part of, as well as managing and developing, a successful and productive team and thrives in highly pressurised and challenging working environments.

OBJECTIVE

Currently looking for a new and challenging position in the civilian logistics arena, one that will make best use of existing skills and experience whilst enabling further personal and professional development.

EDUCATION AND QUALIFICATIONS

CILT:	Advanced Diploma in Logistics & Transport Level 6 (ongoing)
	Professional Diploma in Logistics & Transport (NVQ Level 5/Degree) (2008)
NVQ:	Distribution Warehousing Operations Level 3
	Warehousing Wholesaling Storage Level 2

AFFILIATIONS

- Chartered Institute of Logistics & Transport (MILT)
- Chartered Institute of Leadership & Management (MinstLM)
- European Logistics Association (ESLog)

KEY IT SKILLS

- Word, Excel, PowerPoint, Internet and Email

CAREER SUMMARY

1987–2009   ROYAL AIR FORCE

2006–2009   Logistics Manager

- Managing the procurement of all fuels, lubricants and associated aviation products utilising computerised Inventory Management Systems
- Playing a key role in the overall strategic direction of the department with the focus on achieving demanding KPIs and SLAs
- Working in close conjunction with external agencies to ensure that sufficient inventory levels are maintained in accordance with customer demands with total stock values in excess of £15 million
- Utilising Enterprise Resource Planning databases to maintain strict control over inventory levels and to ensure asset integrity

Key Achievement

- Spearheading the implementation of a Lean event within the department resulting in savings in inventory costs and labour hours by removing non-value adding activities from each work process

CAREER SUMMARY cont.

2003–2006   Logistics Manager – Search & Rescue (SAR)
- Senior Supply Representative and Logistics Specialist supporting Search & Rescue (SAR) operations across the eastern region of the UK whilst simultaneously fulfilling client's logistical requirements
- Responsible for ensuring that sufficient fuel levels are maintained within the supply depot in order to satisfy demand
- Maintaining optimum levels of aircraft inventory with a stock value in excess of £30 million and undertaking accounting procedures in accordance with National Audit Office policy
- Facilitating the timely expedition of aircraft critical assets for transportation and distribution throughout the UK and overseas
- Line managing other staff within the division including dealing with welfare issues and facilitating their career development
- Overseeing the testing of lifecycle products in conjunction with test laboratories and maintaining a first-in, first-out policy of unit stock

Key Achievement
- Developing and implementing a maintenance programme for an old bulk fuel storage depot to enable it to meet stringent quality, health & safety and petroleum standards

2000–2003   Direct Support Manager
- Playing a pivotal role as the primary interface between the RAF, British Aerospace and the Royal Saudi Air Force (RSAF) to ensure that procurement requests from the RSAF are fulfilled
- Periodically reviewing the activities of the prime contractor to ensure that performance levels are maintained in accordance with SLAs
- Liaising extensively between the three agencies to ensure a constant flow of information in order to meet and exceed KPIs
- Coordinating the timely expedition of high value inventory to overseas destinations in accordance with customer deadlines and requirements
- Controlling the sale and loan of high value equipment to the RSAF under the terms of the Al-Yamamah government led project
- Participating in high level meetings to provide advice to respective agencies regarding all aspects of logistics and procurement

Key Achievement
- Successfully reducing aircraft on the ground demands for the client whilst simultaneously selling 2,000 assets to the client resulting in £2.5 million being recouped by the RAF

1991–2000   Logistician – Royal Air Force, Leeds

PERSONAL DETAILS

Driving Licence: Full/Clean
Health: Excellent; non-smoker
Interests include: Sports, Computers, Music and Siberian Huskies

REFERENCES ARE AVAILABLE ON REQUEST

PART 9

MY FIVE TOP TIPS TO MAKE YOUR CV STAND OUT

Chapter **24**

How to make your CV stand out!

If you only had time to read two pages of *The CV Book*, these are the pages I would most like you to have taken the time to read. See them as a 'cheat sheet' as they encapsulate the most important principles that I have covered in the book. Make an effort to accommodate all these when writing your CV and you'll immediately be well above average.

1 Make it readable

It is essential for your CV to be easy for the reader to scan quickly and effectively. You need to separate different sections and insert clear section headings. Avoid long paragraphs; use bullet pointing to break up text into more manageable 'bite-size' chunks. It should be eye-catching and uncluttered. Check vigilantly for spelling and grammatical errors.

2 Include a *Professional profile* and *Objective*

These sections should summarise and emphasise your key attributes and your intended future career path. Your words must flow seamlessly, avoiding cliché and hyperbole.

3 Include *Achievements* where possible

If you can include an *Achievements* section then it can make an instant and dramatic difference to the power of your CV, enabling you to distinguish yourself from other candidates.

4 Keep it concise and to the point

Your CV should be informative and concise. Too many CVs are too long; two A4 pages is the maximum. Only include information which will actually help to sell you. Recruiters don't want to waste time reading details irrelevant to your ability to fulfil the job role.

5 Tailor your CV

If possible, tailor your CV according to the specific vacancy for which you are applying. A carefully targeted CV can easily mean the difference between success and failure.

Conclusion

Writing a CV is not rocket science! Most of what I have outlined is reasonably simple to take on board, so it's just a matter of putting in the necessary time and effort.

I hope you have found *The CV Book* useful. Don't forget to visit our website: **www.jamesinn.es**

GOOD LUCK!

What did you think of this book?

We're really keen to hear from you about this book, so that we can make our publishing even better.

Please log on to the following website and leave us your feedback.

It will only take a few minutes and your thoughts are invaluable to us.

www.pearsoned.co.uk/bookfeedback

Further reading and resources

Recommended books

Borg, J. (2013) *Body Language*, 3rd edition, Harlow: Pearson
Borg, J. (2013) *Persuasion: The Art of Influencing People*, 4th edition, Harlow: Pearson
Edenborough, R. (2009) *Brilliant Psychometric Tests*, Harlow: Pearson
Fagan, A. (2011) *Brilliant Job Hunting*, 3rd edition, Harlow: Pearson
Hall, R. (2010) *The Secrets of Success at Work*, 2nd edition, Harlow: Pearson
Hodgson, S. (2007) *Brilliant Tactics to Pass Aptitude Tests*, 2nd edition, Harlow: Pearson
Innes, J. (2015) *The Cover Letter Book*, 3rd edition, Harlow: Pearson
Innes, J. (2015) *The Interview Book*, 3rd edition, Harlow: Pearson
Innes, J. (2015) *The Interview Question & Answer Book*, 2nd edition, Harlow: Pearson
Innes, J. (2012) *Ultimate New Job*, London: Kogan Page
Johnson, S. (2013) *Brilliant Word 2013*, Harlow: Pearson
Taylor, N. (2011) *Brilliant Business Writing*, 2nd edition, Harlow: Pearson
Templar, R. (2012) *The Rules of Work*, 3rd edition, Harlow: Pearson
Yeung, R. (2013) *Confidence*, 3rd edition, Harlow: Pearson

These titles are available from all major bookshops. You can also learn more about them and place an order for a copy by visiting our website: **www.jamesinn.es**

Online resources

I keep my list of online resources online. That way I can keep it bang up-to-date at all times. Please access our website for a wide range of useful links to job sites and other online resources: **www.jamesinn.es**

Appendix **A**

250 action verbs

Accomplished	Composed	Earned
Achieved	Compounded	Edited
Acquired	Conceived	Educated
Administered	Conducted	Effected
Advised	Conserved	Elected
Advocated	Consolidated	Eliminated
Analysed	Constructed	Employed
Anticipated	Consulted	Enabled
Appointed	Contributed	Encouraged
Appraised	Controlled	Enforced
Approved	Converted	Engineered
Arbitrated	Convinced	Enjoyed
Arranged	Coordinated	Ensured
Articulated	Corrected	Established
Assembled	Corresponded	Estimated
Assessed	Counselled	Evaluated
Assisted	Created	Examined
Attained	Criticised	Exceeded
Audited		Executed
Augmented	Dealt	Expanded
Authorised	Debated	Expedited
Averted	Decided	Explained
Avoided	Decreased	Explored
	Defined	Extracted
Balanced	Delegated	
Began	Delivered	Facilitated
Bought	Demonstrated	Forecast
Briefed	Designated	Formed
Budgeted	Designed	Formulated
Built	Detected	Fostered
	Determined	Founded
Calculated	Developed	Functioned
Captured	Devised	
Centralised	Diagnosed	Gained
Changed	Diminished	Galvanised
Clarified	Directed	Gathered
Classified	Discovered	Generated
Coached	Dispensed	Guided
Collated	Disproved	
Collected	Distributed	Handled
Combined	Documented	Heightened
Communicated	Doubled	Highlighted
Completed	Dropped	Hired

Identified
Implemented
Improved
Improvised
Increased
Initiated
Inspected
Inspired
Installed
Instigated
Instituted
Instructed
Interacted
Introduced
Invented
Investigated

Launched
Led
Liaised
Liquidated
Located
Logged

Maintained
Managed
Mapped
Marketed
Maximised
Mediated
Modernised
Modified
Monitored
Motivated

Named
Navigated
Negotiated
Networked

Observed
Obtained

Operated
Ordered
Organised
Originated
Oversaw

Participated
Perceived
Performed
Pioneered
Placed
Planned
Positioned
Prepared
Prescribed
Presented
Prevailed
Prevented
Prioritised
Processed
Procured
Produced
Profited
Programmed
Promoted
Protected
Proved
Provided
Published
Purchased

Raised
Ran
Rated
Realised
Received
Recognised
Recommended
Reconciled
Recorded
Recruited
Redesigned

Reduced
Referred
Regulated
Rejected
Related
Rendered
Reorganised
Represented
Researched
Resolved
Restored
Reviewed
Revised
Revitalised
Routed

Saved
Scheduled
Scrutinised
Selected
Sent
Served
Settled
Shaped
Simplified
Sold
Solved
Specified
Staffed
Standardised
Stimulated
Streamlined
Strengthened
Studied
Supervised
Supplied
Supported
Surpassed
Surveyed

Targeted
Taught

Terminated
Tested
Tightened
Traded

Trained
Transformed
Tripled

Vitalised

Wrote

Appendix **B**

50 positive adjectives

Able
Accurate
Adaptable
Analytical
Articulate
Astute

Consistent
Creative

Decisive
Dedicated
Diligent
Diplomatic
Dynamic

Effective
Efficient
Energetic
Enthusiastic
Experienced

Fast
Flexible

Gregarious

Imaginative
Innovative
Inventive

Methodical
Motivated

Organised
Outgoing
Outstanding

Patient
Perceptive
Persistent
Positive
Practical

Productive
Proficient
Punctual

Quick

Rational
Reliable
Resourceful
Responsible

Self-motivated
Self-reliant
Shrewd
Strong
Successful

Tactful
Talented

Versatile

Appendix **C**

222 commonly misspelled words

Absence
Acceptable
Accidentally
Accommodate
Achieve
Acquire
Acquit
Address
Advertise
Advice
Alternative
Amongst
Analysis
Apparent
Argument

Balance
Basically
Becoming
Before
Beginning
Believe
Benefit
Brilliant
Bureaucracy
Business

Calendar
Careful
Caribbean
Category
Ceiling
Certain
Changeable
Coming
Committed
Committee
Competition
Concurring
Confidential
Conglomerate
Conscience
Conscientious

Conscious
Consensus
Constituents
Contravene
Controversy
Convenience
Credentials

Decide
Definite
Definitely
Deliberate
Describe
Deterrence
Development
Difference
Dilemma
Disappear
Discipline
Discovery
Distributors
Does
During

Easily
Eight
Either
Eligible
Entrepreneur
Environment
Equipment
Equipped
Exaggerate
Exceed
Excellent
Except
Exclusive
Exercise
Existence
Expect
Experience
Experiment
Explanation

Familiar
Fascinating
Finally
Foreign
Forward
Fulfil
Fundamental

Gauge
Generally
Government
Guarantee
Guidance

Height
Hierarchy
Humorous

Identity
Imitate
Imitation
Immediate
Immediately
Improvement
Incidentally
Incredible
Independent
Indispensable
Influential
Integrated
Interesting
Interfere
Interpretation
Interruption
Irrelevant
Irritable

Knowledge

Legislation
Leisure
Length
Lesson

Liaison
Library
Losing

Maintenance
Miniature
Minute
Misspell

Naturally
Necessary
Neither
Noticeable

Occasion
Occasionally
Occurred
Occurrence
Official
Often
Omission
Operate
Optimism
Original

Parallel
Particularly
Perceive
Perform
Permanent
Perseverance
Persevere
Personally
Personnel
Persuade
Picture
Piece
Planning

Political
Possible
Practical
Precede
Prefer
Prejudice
Presence
Principal
Privilege
Probably
Proceed
Professional
Promise
Psychology
Publicly

Quantity
Quarter
Questionnaire
Queue
Quite

Receipt
Receive
Recommend
Reference
Referrals
Referred
Relevant
Repetition
Restaurant

Sacrifice
Safety
Scenario
Schedule
Secretary
Seize

Semantics
Separate
Shining
Similar
Sincerely
Solution
Speech
Stopping
Strength
Studying
Succeed
Successful
Supersede
Surely
Surprise
Syndicate
Systematic

Temperature
Temporary
Threshold
Through
Tomorrow
Toward
Tries
Truly
Twelfth

Unnecessary
Until
Unusual
Usually

Warrantee
Whether
Writing

Index